EASY RUSSIAN PHRASE BOOK

Over 1500 Common Phrases For Everyday Use And Travel

www.LingoMastery.com

ISBN: 978-1-951949-15-0

Free Book Reveals The 6 Step Blueprint That Took Students **from Language Learners To Fluent In 3 Months**

- **6 Unbelievable Hacks** that will accelerate your learning curve
- **Mind Training:** why memorizing vocabulary is easy
- **One Hack To Rule Them All:** This <u>secret nugget</u> will blow you away...

Head over to **LingoMastery.com/hacks**
and claim your free book now!

CONTENTS

INTRODUCTION

If you have finally decided to visit Russia, one of the richest countries in history and culture, then you should naturally be thinking about the words, phrases, and essential things that a variety of everyday situations call for. This is all the more important since, unfortunately, the average level of English comprehension in Russia is not that good when compared to other European countries.

Thanks to this book, we will learn how to address many situations that can be simple, complicated, funny, or not so funny at all – all those real circumstances that a tourist would experience when, for example, looking for activities , ordering dishes with national cuisine at a restaurant, or simply don't want to be bothered.

Think of the souvenirs you would bring back for a relative: do you want to negotiate your price or ask for a discount? In that case, it is certain that you will need to express yourself correctly.

Most of the time, having the vocabulary at your fingertips is the best solution, so why not take precautions and study a few phrases that could amaze your fellow travelers or your future conversation partners?

Of course, there are some obstacles to overcome, and the greatest one is pronunciation. Let's see what letters there are in the Russian language and what sounds they produce. The Cyrillic alphabet, which is the alphabet the Russian language uses, may look intimidating at first, but we promise it isn't nearly as intimidating as it seems to you right now.

Also please note that we capitalize stressed syllables for your convenience. For example, 'мама' (mom) – [MA-ma]. If there are no capitalized syllables, then it means that there is only one syllable in the word.

Each sentence is followed by a detailed transcription. At first you may be slow at 'decoding' it, but don't get discouraged if it sounds difficult or you stumble over certain letters. It is all part of the process, and if you

1

are patient and attentive, you will be faster and faster with every next word.

Pronunciation of Russian vowels

There are ten letters in the Russian language that are used to indicate vowels: А, О, У, Э, Ы, И, Е, Ё, Ю, Я.

Let's see how they are pronounced and how they will be transcribed in transcription in this book. The first five, the hard vowels, are quite simple.

А – [a], pronounced as a pure 'ah', or the sound you make when your doctor tells you to stick your tongue out (or the 'a' in 'father') – [a]. In unstressed syllables it can be pronounced as a neutral vowel, just like the first and third syllables in the word 'banana'– [ə].

О – [o], pronounced like 'o' in 'toe'. In unstressed syllables it can be pronounced either as the previous [a] sound or as a neutral vowel – [ə].

У – [u], pronounced like 'oo' in 'moon' but not so much prolonged. Sometimes can be pronounced as a neutral vowel – [ə].

Э – [eh], like the 'e' in 'bed'.

There is one more hard vowel that we don't have in English: *Ы – [y].* This sound is usually difficult for Russian learners to understand and pronounce. To get an idea of how to do it, try to hold the long [i:] vowel sound in the word "be". Feel the sides of your tongue touching the insides of your top molars? Keep the sides of your tongue exactly where they are and slowly drop the center of your tongue. If it sounds and feels goofy, don't worry – it should. Tried it?

So, this is how Russian 'ы' is pronounced. Or, there is also another way. When you pronounce the long [i:] sound, the root of your tongue goes down, while the tip of the tongue goes to your lower teeth. With the Russian [y] sound you should do everything the other way around – the root of the tongue goes up, while the tip of the tongue doesn't touch the teeth at all.

For example, 'мы' (we) – [my].

Next, let's move on to the soft vowels. For now, just think of soft vowels as hard vowels with a [j] in front of them. The sound [j] corresponds to the English 'y' in 'yes'.

In fact, the sound [j] is always considered to be a separate syllable in Russian phonetics, but to make it easier for you to unite sounds into words, we've decided to mark the combinations of [j] and vowels as one syllable.

Я – [j+a], pronounced like the 'ya' in 'y'all'.

For example, 'рядом' (next to) – [R'A-dəm] and 'яхта' (yacht) – [JA-h-tə]

Ё – [j+o], pronounced like the word 'yo'.

For example, 'лёд' (ice) – [l'od] and 'ёж' (hedgehog) – [josh]

Ю – [j+u], pronounced like the word 'you'.

For example, 'люди' (people) – [L'U-d'i] and 'юг' (south) – [juk]

Е – [j+eh], pronounced like the 'ye' in 'yellow'.

For example, 'лето' (summer) – [L'EH-tə] and 'ель' (fir tree) – [jehl']

И – [i], pronounced like 'ee' in 'knee' but not so prolonged.

That's all the vowels! Russian pronunciation has some specifics that we will mention here, although don't worry too much about them. If you practice using the pronunciation that we are providing you with, you will certainly be understood by Russian speakers!

That said, the letters (Е, Ё, Ю, Я) can be pronounced in different ways depending on what other letters surround them.

These vowels can produce two sounds if they are located:

- At the beginning of the sentence
- After a vowel
- After 'ь' (the soft sign) or 'ъ' (the hard sign). These letters are read but not pronounced. They only point out the softness or hardness of the preceding letter.

In all the other places they have one sound.

*****

The following vowels make the preceding hard consonant soft – e, ё, ю, я, и.

For example, 'лес' (forest) – *[l'ehs]*

For Russian native speakers it is natural to observe this softness even if they don't know this phonetics rule. But since you are not a native speaker, we've marked all the soft consonants for you so that you don't have to focus on remembering the rule and applying it.

Again, don't worry too much about this at the start. We are telling you how to pronounce everything correctly anyway!

Ready to go over to consonants? They are simple, we promise! Let's start with letters that look exactly the same.

К – *[k]*

Pronounced like 'c' in 'cat'; unlike in English the sound is never aspirated.

М – *[m]*

Pronounced like 'm' in 'milk'.

Т – *[t]*

Pronounced like 't' in 'tiger', but with your tongue on your teeth and not on your palate (like we say in English).

Now let's take a look at the letters that will be totally new to you (even if the sounds themselves won't be)!

П – *[p]*

Like 'p' in 'pipe', unlike in English the sound is never aspirated.

Л – *[l]*

Pronounced like 'l' in 'lemon', but with your tongue on your teeth and not on your palate (like we say in English).

Г – *[g]*

Pronounced like 'g' in 'get'.

Д – [d]

Pronounced like 'd' in 'dear', but with your tongue on your teeth and not on your palate (like we say in English).

Ф – [f]

Pronounced like [f] in 'film', just a bit more relaxed.

Ч – [ch]

Pronounced like 'ch' in 'chicken'.

Й – [j]

Pronounced like 'y' in 'yoga'.

Ц – [ts]

Pronounced like the combination of the sounds [t] and [s].

Ж – [zh]

This sound is a bit special. To understand how to pronounce it, think of the second 'g' in the word 'garage'. The consonant you get is [zh]. For example, 'жена' (wife) – [zheh-NA]

Ш – [sh]

Pronounced like 'sh' in 'shy'.

Щ – [sch]

Pronounced like the combination of [s] and [ch] sounds.

Б – [b]

Pronounced like 'b' in 'bear'.

Great! Now let's look at the tricky letters, as in the letters whose sounds don't correlate to what we would expect as English speakers.

В – [v]

Pronounced like 'v' in 'video', but not as intense.

З – [z]

Pronounced like 'z' in 'zoo'.

Н – [n]

Pronounced like 'n' in 'nose', but with your tongue on your teeth and not on your palate.

Р – [r]

Pronounced like 'r' in 'river', but the tip of your tongue should be on the front part of your palate and not on the back one like in English. There is no rolling 'r' in Russian either.

С – [s]

Pronounced like 's' in snow, but with your tongue on your teeth and not on your palate.

Х – [h]

Pronounced like 'h' in 'home'.

And last but not least, the true black sheep of the Cyrillic alphabet – the hard and soft signs. Again, these letters are read but not pronounced. They only point out the softness or hardness of the preceding letter.

ь

Produces no sound, just makes the preceding consonant soft. For example, 'семь' (seven) – [s'ehm'] – think about making the 'm' smaller when you pronounce this.

ъ

Produces no sound, just makes the preceding consonant hard. For example, 'объём' (volume) – [ab-JOM] – make that [j] sound nice and big!

*****

There are voiced and voiceless consonants.

The following consonants are always voiced –

[l] (л),
[m] (м),
[n] (н),
[r] (р),
[j] (й).

The following consonants are always voiceless –

[h] (х),
[ts] (ц),
[ch] (ч),
[sch] (щ).

The rest form voiced/voiceless pairs:

[b] (б)/[p] (п)
[d] (д)/[t] (т)
[z] (з)/[s] (с)
[g] (г)/[k] (к)
[v] (в)/[f] (ф)
[zh] (ж)/[sh] (ш)

Depending on the position in a word, these voiced consonants can become voiceless and vice versa.

Voiced consonants become voiceless when

- They stand at the end of a word. For example, 'боб' (bean) should be pronounced [bop], because the [b] becomes a [p].
- They are followed by a voiceless consonant. For example, 'Ложка' (spoon) should be pronounced [LO-shka], because the [zh] becomes a [sh].

Voiceless consonants become voiced when they are followed by voiced consonants.

For example, 'просьба' [request] is pronounced [PRO-z'ba] because the [s] becomes a [z].

*****

Other useful notes:

- In Russian, verbs and pronouns can have different gender forms, which means men and women use slightly different versions of the same words to say the same things. When this is the case, we've included both male and female forms for you and separated them with a slash.

  For example, 'I would like a cup of tea' – 'Я бы <u>хотел</u>/**хотела** чашечку чая' – 'Ja by <u>ha-T'EHL</u>/**ha-T'EH-la** CHA-sheh-chku CHA-ja.'

  The underlined form of the verb is what men would say to ask for a cup of tea, and the bold form is what women would say to do the same.

- The pronoun 'you' can be translated into Russian either as 'ты', [ty] or 'вы' [vy]. The latter form, [vy], is more official and is more suitable for official situations as well as for talking to strangers, whereas [ty] is accepted between friends and occasionally between acquaintances of the same age group. When choosing which form to include in the translation, we were guided by the desire to help you sound as appropriate as possible, as the distinction between the two carries social significance in Russian. Of course, there are cases when both forms can be used, but we don't want you to risk sounding rude, so we used the informal 'you' only when it is 100% recommended to do so.
- You will come across many words that were borrowed from the English language. In some cases, Russian people pronounce them just like we do in English, and in those situations, we didn't include the transcription for such words (for example, 'GPS').
- The verb 'to be' in the Present tense is implicit in Russian grammar. What on earth does that mean, though? Basically, any time we use the verb 'to be' in the Present tense in English, (i.e. "I am hungry.", "This backpack is blue.") Russians understand it through context (literally saying "I hungry." and "This backpack blue.") Don't worry if it seems like Russian uses fewer words than English!

8

- Russian grammar also does not have articles ("the", "a/an"). Whereas in English we'd say "The Diner was a nice restaurant!", the Russians literally say "Diner was nice restaurant!"
- Russian grammar is very, very complicated for many reasons. One reason is that all nouns and adjectives have gender that most learners have to memorize individually. Lucky for you, we did all the work! When reading the phrases in this book, just bear in mind that endings in words often change in Russian. Consider the following example: The sky is **blue** / Небо **синее** / *N'EH-bə **S'I-n'eh-jeh***. The color 'blue' has to agree with the word 'sky', which in Russian is gendered neutrally. In a similar sentence, we see a slight change: That paint is **blue** / Эта краска **синяя** / *EH-tə KRAS-kа **S'I-n'a-ja***. Because our adjectives in English don't change, the word 'blue' is the same in both sentences. However, in Russian, the word 'blue' has to agree with the feminine noun 'paint', and so it looks just a little different.

Well, now you know how to read Russian letters and pronounce them correctly. Time to put your knowledge into practice! We welcome you to start your journey with this Easy Russian Phrase Book!

COLORS

Gold
Золотой
Za-la-TOJ

Red
Красный
KRAS-nyj

Orange
Оранжевый
A-RAN-zheh-vyj

Yellow
Жёлтый
ZH'OL-tyj

Green
Зелёный
Z'eh-L'O-nyj

Blue
Синий
S'I-n'ij

Light blue
Голубой
Ga-lu-BOJ

Violet
Фиолетовый
Fi-a-L'EH-ta-vyj

Pink
Розовый
RO-zə-vyj

Brown
Коричневый
Ka-R'ICH-n'eh-vyj

Purple
Пурпурный
Pur-PUR-nyj

White
Белый
B'Eh-lyj

Black
Чёрный
CH'OR-nyj

Gray
Серый
S'Eh-ryj

Silver
Серебристый
S'eh-r'ehb-R'I-styj

What color is that sign?
Какого цвета этот знак?
Ka-KO-və TSV'Eh-ta EH-tət znak?

Is the cartoon in color?

Этот мультфильм цветной?
EH-tət mul't-F'IL'M tsv'eht-NOJ?

Is this television show in color?
Эта передача в цвете?
EH-ta p'eh-r'eh-DA-cha f TSV'EH-t'eh?

This is a red pen.
Это красная ручка.
EH-tə KRAS-na-ja RU-chka.

This piece of paper is blue.
Этот листок бумаги синий.
EH-tət l'is-TOK bu-MA-g'i S'I-n'ij.

What color is that car?
Какого цвета эта машина?
Ka-KO-və TSV'EH-ta EH-ta ma-SHY-na?

What color are your clothes?
Какого цвета твоя одежда?
Ka-KO-və TSV'EH-ta tva-JA a-D'EHZH-da?

Is this the right color?
Это правильный цвет?
EH-tə PRA-v'il'-nyj tsv'eht?

What color is the stop light?
Какого цвета сигнал светофора?
Ka-KO-və TSV'EH-ta s'ig-NAL sv'eh-ta-FO-ra?

Does that color mean danger?
Этот цвет означает опасность?
EH-tət tsv'eht az-na-CHA-jeht a-PA-snəst'?

That bird is red.
Эта птица красная.
EH-ta PT'I-tsa KRAS-na-ja.

What color is that animal?
Какого цвета это животное?
Ka-KO-və TSV'EH-ta EH-tə zhy-VOT-nə-jeh?

The sky is blue.
Небо синее.
N'EH-bə S'I-n'eh-jeh.

The clouds are white.
Облака белые.
Ab-la-KA B'EH-ly-jeh.

That paint is blue.
Эта краска синяя.
EH-tə KRAS-ka S'I-n'a-ja.

11

Press the red button.
Нажмите на красную кнопку.
Nazh-M'I-t'eh na KRAS-nu-ju KNOP-ku.

Don't press the red button.
Не нажимайте на красную кнопку.
N'eh na-zhy-MAJ-t'eh na KRAS-nu-ju KNOP-ku.

Black and White.
Чёрно-белый.
TCH'OR-nə-B'EH-lyj.

Look at all the colors.
Посмотрите на все цвета.
Pas-mat-R'I-t'eh na fs'eh tsv'eh-TA.

Is that a color television?
Это цветной телевизор?
EH-tə tsv'eht-NOJ t'eh-l'eh-V'I-zər?

What color do you see?
Какой цвет вы видите?
Ka-KOJ tsv'eht vy V'I-d'i-t'eh?

Can I have the color blue?
Можно мне синий цвет?
MO-zhna mn'eh S'I-n'ij tsv'eht ?

What color do you have for these frames?
В каком цвете у вас есть эти рамки?
F ka-KOM TSV'EH-t'eh u vas jehst' EH-t'i RAM-k'i?

Don't go until the color is green.
Не идите, пока не загорится зелёный.
N'eh i-D'I-t'eh pa-KA n'eh za-ga-R'I-tsa z'eh-L'O-nyj.

Colored pencils.
Цветные карандаши.
Tsv'eht-NY-jeh ka-ran-da-SHY.

Colored pens.
Цветные ручки.
Tsv'eht-NY-jeh RU-chk'i.

The sharpie is black.
Маркер чёрный.
MAR-k'ehr CH'OR-nyj.

I passed with flying colors.
Я сдал/сдала на «отлично».
Ja zdal/zda-LA na at-L'ICH-nə.

Do you have this in another color?
У вас есть это в другом цвете?
U vas jehst' EH-tə v dru-GOM TSV'EH-t'eh?

Do you have this in a darker color?
У вас есть это в более тёмном цвете?
U vas jehst' EH-tə v BO-l'eh-jeh T'OM-nəm TSV'Eh-t'eh?

Do you have this in a lighter color?
У вас есть это в более светлом цвете?
U vas jehst' EH-tə v BO-l'e-jeh SV'EHT-ləm TSV'EH-t'eh?

Can you paint my house blue?
Вы можете покрасить мой дом в синий цвет?
Vy MO-zheh-t'eh pak-RA-s'it' moj dom f S'I-n'ij tsv'eht?

Can you paint my car the same color?
Вы можете покрасить мою машину в тот же цвет?

Vy MO-zheh-t'eh pak-RA-s'it' ma-JU ma-SHY-nu f tot zheh tsv'eht?

The flag has three different colors.
На флаге три разных цвета.
Na FLA-g'eh tr'i RAZ-nyh TSV'EH-ta.

Is the color on the flag red?
Цвет на флаге красный?
Tsv'eht na FLA-g'eh KRAS-nyj?

NUMBERS

Zero
Ноль
Nol'

One
Один
a-D'IN

Two
Два
Dva

Three
Три
Tr'i

Four
Четыре
Ch'eh-TY-r'eh

Five
Пять
P'at'

Six
Шесть
Shehst'

Seven
Семь
S'ehm'

Eight
Восемь
VO-s'ehm'

Nine
Девять
D'EH-v'at'

Ten
Десять
D'EH-s'at'

Eleven
Одиннадцать
A-D'I-na-tsat'

Twelve
Двенадцать
Dv'eh-NA-tsat'

Thirteen
Тринадцать
Tr'i-NA-tsat'

Fourteen
Четырнадцать
Ch'eh-TYR-na-tsat'

Fifteen
Пятнадцать
P'at-NA-tsat'

Sixteen
Шестнадцать
Shehs-NA-tsat'

Seventeen
Семнадцать
S'ehm-NA-tsat'

Eighteen
Восемнадцать
Va-s'ehm-NA-tsat'

Nineteen
Девятнадцать
D'eh-v'at-NA-tsat'

Twenty
Двадцать
DVA-tsat'

Twenty-one
Двадцать один
DVA-tsat' a-D'IN

Twenty-two
Двадцать два
DVA-tsat' dva

Twenty-three
Двадцать три
DVA-tsat' tr'i

Twenty-four
Двадцать четыре
DVA-tsat' Ch'eh-TY-r'eh

Twenty-five
Двадцать пять
DVA-tsat' p'at'

Twenty-six
Двадцать шесть
DVA-tsat' shehst'

Twenty-seven
Двадцать семь
DVA-tsat' s'ehm'

Twenty-eighth
Двадцать восемь
DVA-tsat' VO-s'ehm'

Twenty-n'ine
Двадцать девять
DVA-tsat' D'EH-v'at'

Thirty
Тридцать
TR'I-tsat'

Forty
Сорок
SO-rək

Fifty
Пятьдесят
P'at'-d'eh-S'AT

Sixty
Шестьдесят
Shehst'-d'eh-S'AT

Seventy
Семьдесят
S'EHM'-d'eh-s'at

Eighty
Восемьдесят
VO-s'ehm-d'eh-s'at

Ninety
Девяноста
D'eh-v'a-NOS-tə

One hundred
Сто
Sto

Two hundred
Двести
DV'EH-st'i

Five hundred
Пятьсот
P'at'-SOT

One thousand
Тысяча
TY-s'a-cha

One hundred thousand
Сто тысяч
Sto TY-s'ach

One million
Один миллион
a-D'IN m'i-l'i-ON

One billion
Один миллиард
a-D'IN m'i-l'i-ARD

What does that add up to?
Сколько получается?
SKOL'-kə pa-lu-CHA-jeh-tsa?

What number is on this paper?
Какая цифра написана на этой бумаге?
Ka-KA-ja TSYF-ra na-P'I-sa-na na EH-təj bu-MA-g'eh?

What number is on this sign?
Какая цифра стоит на этом знаке?
Ka-KA-ja TSYF-ra sta-IT na EH-təm ZNA-k'eh?

Are these two numbers equal?
Эти два числа равны?
EH-t'i dva ch'is-LA rav-NY?

My social security number is one, two, three, four, five.
Номер моего социального страхования — один, два, три, четыре, пять.
NO-m'ehr ma-jeh-VO sa-tsy-AL'-nə-və stra-ha-VA-n'i-ja — a-D'IN, dva, tr'I, ch'eh-TY-r'eh, p'at'.

I'm going to bet five thousand euros.
Я ставлю пять тысяч евро.
Ja STAV-l'u p'at' TY-s'ach' JEHV-rə.

Can you count to one hundred for me?
Ты можешь посчитать мне до ста?
Ty MO-zhehsh pas-ch'i-TAT' mn'eh də sta?

I took fourteen steps.
Я прошёл/прошла четырнадцать шагов.
Ja pra-SHOL /prash-LA ch'eh-TYR-na-tsat' sha-GOF.

I ran two kilometers.
Я пробежал/пробежала два километра.
Ja pra-b'eh-ZHAL/pra-b'eh-ZHA-la dva k'i-la-M'EHT-ra.

The speed limit is 30 km/h.
Ограничение скорости — тридцать километров в час.
Ag-ra-n'i-CH'EH-n'i-jeh SKO-ras-t'i — TR'I-tsat' k'i-la-M'EHT-rəf f chas.

What are the measurements?
Какие размеры?
Ka-K'I-jeh raz-M'EH-ry?

Can you dial this number?
Вы можете набрать этот номер?
Vy MO-zheh-t'eh nab-RAT' EH-tət NO-m'her?

One dozen.
Одна дюжина.
A-DNA D'U-zhy-na.

A half dozen.
Полдюжины.
Pol-D'U-zhy-ny.

How many digits are in the number?
Сколько цифр в этом номере?
SKOL'-kə tsyfr v EH-təm NO-m'eh-r'eh?

My phone number is nine, eight, five, six, two, one, eight, seven, eight, eight.

Мой номер телефона — девять, восемь, пять, шесть, два, один, восемь, семь, восемь, восемь.

Moj NO-m'ehr t'eh'l'eh-FO-na — D'EH-v'at', VO-s'ehm', shehst', dva, a-D'IN, VO-s'ehm', s'ehm', VO-s'ehm', VO-s'ehm'.

The hotel's phone number is one, eight hundred, three, two, three, five, seven, five, five.

Номер отеля — один, восемь, три, два, три, пять, семь, пять, пять.

NO-m'ehr a-TEH-l'a — a-D'IN, VO-s'ehm', t'ri, dva, tr'i, p'at', s'ehm', p'at', p'at'.

The taxi number is six, eight, one, four, four, four, five, eight, one, nine.

Номер такси — шесть, восемь, один, четыре, четыре, четыре, пять, восемь, один, девять.

NO-m'ehr tak-SI — shehst', VO-s'ehm', a-D'IN, ch'eh-TY-r'eh, ch'eh-TY-r'eh, ch'eh-TY-r'eh, p'at', VO-s'ehm', a-D'IN, D'EH-v'at'.

Call my hotel at two, one, four, seven, one, two, nine, five, seven, six.

Позвони в мой отель по номеру два, один, четыре, семь, один, два, девять, пять, семь, шесть.

Pa-zva-N'I v moj a-TEHL' pə NO-m'eh-ru dva, a-D'IN, ch'eh-TY-r'eh, s'ehm', a-D'IN, dva, D'EH-v'at', p'at', s'ehm', shehst'.

Call the embassy at nine, eight, nine, eight, four, three, two, one, seven, one.

Позвоните в посольство по номеру девять, восемь, девять, восемь, четыре, три, два, один, семь, один.

Pa-z-va-N'I-t'eh f pa-SOL'-stvə pə NO-m'eh-ru D'EH-v'at', VO-s'ehm', D'EH-v'at', VO-s'ehm', cheh-TY-r'eh, tr'i, dva, a-D'IN, s'ehm', a-D'IN.

GREETINGS

Hi!
Привет!

Pr'i-V'EHT!

How's it going?
Как дела?

Kak d'eh-LA?

What's new?
Что нового?

Shto NO-və-və?

What's going on?
Что происходит?
Shto pra-is-HO-d'it?

Home, sweet home.
Родной дом.
Rad-NOJ dom.

Ladies and gentlemen, thank you for coming.
Дамы и господа, спасибо, что пришли.
DA-my i gas-pa-DA, spa-S'I-bə, shto pr'ish-L'I.

How is everything?
Как жизнь?
Kak zhyzn'?

Long time, no see.
Давно не виделись.
Dav-NO n'eh V'I-d'eh-l'is'.

It's been a long time.
Сколько лет, сколько зим!
SKOL'-kə l'eht, SKOL'-kə z'im!

It's been a while!
Сколько времени прошло!
SKOL'-kə VR'EH-m'eh-n'i prash-LO!

How is life?
Как жизнь?
Kak zhyzn'?

How is your day?
Как прошёл твой день?
Kak pra-SHOL tvoj d'ehn'?

Good morning.
Доброе утро.
DO-brə-jeh U-trə.

It's been too long!
Я заждался/заждалась!
Ja zazh-DAL-s'a/zazh-da-LAS'!

Good afternoon.
Добрый день.
DOB-ryj d'ehn'.

How long has it been?
Сколько времени прошло?
SKOL'-kə VR'EH-m'eh-n'i prash-LO?

It's a pleasure to meet you.
Приятно познакомиться.
Pr'i-JAT-nə paz-na-KO-m'i-tsa.

It's always a pleasure to see you.
Всегда приятно встретиться с тобой.
Fs'ehg-DA pr'i-JAT-nə FSTR'EH-t'i-tsa s ta-BOJ.

Allow me to introduce Earl, my husband.
Позвольте представить вам моего мужа, Эрла.
Paz-VOL'-t'eh pr'ehd-STA-v'it' vam ma-jeh-VO MU-zha, Ehrla.

Goodnight.
Спокойной ночи.
Spa-KOJ-naj NO-ch'i.

May I introduce my brother and sister?
Могу я представить вам моих брата и сестру?
Ma-GU ja pr'ehd-STA-v'it' vam ma-IH BRA-tə i s'ehs-TRU?

Good evening.
Добрый вечер.
DOB-ryj V'EH-ch'ehr.

What's happening?
Что происходит?
Shto pra-is-HO-d'it?

Happy holidays!
С праздником!
S PRAZ-n'i-kəm!

Are you alright?
Вы в порядке?
Vy f pa-R'AT-k'eh?

Merry Christmas!
Весёлого Рождества!
Ve-S'O-lə-və razh-d'eh-STVA!

Where have you been hiding?
Где ты пропадал/пропадала?
Gd'eh ty pra-pa-DAL/pra-pa-DA-la?

Happy New Year!
С Новым Годом!
S NO-vym GO-dəm!

How is your night?
Как проходит ваш вечер?
Kak pra-HO-d'it vash V'EH-ch'ehr?

What have you been up to all these years?
Чем ты занимался/занималась все эти годы?
Ch'ehm ty za-n'i-MAL-s'a/za-n'i-MA-las' fs'eh EH-t'i GO-dy?

When was the last time we saw each other?
Когда мы виделись в последний раз?
Kag-DA my V'I-d'eh-l'is' f pas-L'EHD-n'ij ras?

It's been ages since I've seen you.
Мы с тобой не виделись сто лет.
My s ta-BOJ n'eh V'I-d'eh-l'is' sto l'eht.

How have things been going since I saw you last?
Что у тебя нового, с тех пор как мы виделись в последний раз?
Shto u t'eh-B'A NO-və-və s t'ehh por kak my V'I-d'eh-l'is' f pas-L'EHD-n'ij raz?

What have you been up to?
Чем ты занимался/занималась в последнее время?
Ch'ehm ty za-n'i-MAL-s'a/-za-n'i-MA-las' f pas-L'EHD-n'eh-jeh VR'EH-m'a?

How are you doing?
Как поживаешь?
Kak pa-zhy-VA-jehsh?

Goodbye.
Пока.
Pa-KA.

Are you okay?
Ты в порядке?
Ty f pa-R'AT-k'eh?

How's life been treating you?
Как жизнь?
Kak zhyzn'?

I'm sorry.
Мне очень жаль.
Mn'eh O-ch'ehn' zhal'.

Excuse me.
Извините.
Iz-v'i-N'I-t'eh.

See you later!
До встречи!
Da FSTR'EH-chi!

What's your name?
Как вас зовут?
Kak vas za-VUT?

My name is Bill.
Меня зовут Билл.

M'eh-N'A za-VUT B'il.

Pleased to meet you.
Приятно познакомиться.
Pr'i-JAT-nə paz-na-KO-m'i-tsa.

How do you do?
Как поживаете?
Kak pa-zhy-VA-jeh-t'eh?

How are things?
Как дела?

Kak d'eh-LA?

You're welcome.
Пожалуйста.

Pa-ZHA-lə-stə.

It's good to see you.
Рад/рада тебя видеть.

Rad/RA-da t'eh-B'A V'I-d'eht'.

How have you been?
Чем ты занимался/занималась в последнее время?
Ch'ehm ty za-n'i-MAL-s'a/za-n'i-MA-las' f pas-L'EHD-n'eh-jeh VR'EH-m'a?

Nice to meet you.
Приятно познакомиться.
Pr'i-JAT-nə paz-na-KO-m'i-tsa.

Fine, thanks. And you?
Спасибо, хорошо. А у тебя?
Spa-S'I-bə, ha-ra-SHO. A u t'eh-B'A?

Good day to you.
Хорошего тебе дня.
Ha-RO-sheh-və t'eh-B'EH dn'a.

Come in, the door is open.
Входи, дверь открыта.
Fha-D'I, dv'ehr' at-KRY-ta.

My wife's name is Sheila.
Мою жену зовут Шейла.
Ma-ju zheh-NU za-VUT SHEHJ-la.

I've been looking for you!
Я искал/искала тебя!
Ja is-KAL/is-KA-la t'eh-B'A!

Allow me to introduce myself. My name is Earl.
Позвольте представиться. Меня зовут Эрл.
Paz-VOL'-t'eh pr'ehd-STA-v'i-tsa. M'eh-N'A za-VUT Ehrl.

I hope you have enjoyed your weekend!
Надеюсь, ты хорошо провёл/провела выходные!
Na-D'EH-jus', ty ha-ra-SHO pra-V'OL/pra-v'eh-LA vy-had-NY-jeh!

It's great to hear from you.
Рад/рада слышать тебя.
Rad/RA-da SLY-shat' t'eh-B'A.

I hope you are having a great day.
Надеюсь, у тебя сегодня отличный день.
Na-D'EH-jus' u t'eh-B'A s'eh-VO-dn'a at-L'ICH-nyj d'ehn'.

Thank you for your help.
Спасибо за помощь.
Spa-S'I-bə za PO-məsch.

DATE AND TIME

January
Январь
Jan-VAR'

February
Февраль
F'ehv-RAL'

March
Март
Mart

April
Апрель
Ap-R'EHL'

May
Май
Maj

June
Июнь
i-JUN'

July
Июль
i-JUL'

August
Август
AV-gust

September
Сентябрь
S'ehn-T'ABR'

October

Октябрь
Ak-T'ABR'

November
Ноябрь
Na-JABR'

December
Декабрь
D'eh-KABR'

What month is it?

Какой сейчас месяц?

Ka-KOJ s'eh-CHAS M'EH-s'ats?

At what time?

Во сколько?

Va SKOL'-kə?

Do you observe Daylight saving time?

Вы переводите часы на зимнее время?

Vy p'eh-r'eh-VO-d'i-t'eh cha-SY na Z'IM-n'eh-jeh VR'EH-m'a?

The current month is January.

Сейчас январь.

S'eh-CHAS jan-VAR'.

What day of the week is it?

Какой сегодня день недели?

Ka-KOJ s'eh-VO-dn'a d'ehn' n'eh-D'EH-l'i?

Is today Tuesday?

Сегодня вторник?

S'eh-VO-dn'a FTOR-n'ik?

Today is Monday.

Сегодня понедельник.

S'eh-VO-dn'a pa-n'eh-D'EHL'-n'ik.

Is this the month of January?

Сейчас январь?

S'eh-CHAS jan-VAR'?

It is five minutes past one.

Сейчас пять минут второго.

S'eh-CHAS p'at' m'i-NUT fta-RO-və.

It is ten minutes past one.

Сейчас десять минут второго.

S'eh-CHAS D'EH-s'at' m'i-NUT fta-RO-və.

It is ten till one.

Сейчас без десяти час.

S'eh-CHAS b'ehz d'eh-s'a-T'I chas.

It is half past one.
Сейчас половина второго.
S'eh-CHAS pa-la-V'I-na fta-RO-və.

What time is it?
Сколько времени?
SKOL'-kə VR'EH-m'eh-n'i?

When does the sun go down?
Во сколько заходит солнце?
Va SKOL'-kə za-HO-d'it SON-tseh?

It's the third of November.
Третье ноября.
TR'EH-tjeh na-jab-R'A.

When does it get dark?
Во сколько темнеет?
Va SKOL'-kə t'ehm-N'EH-jeht?

What is today's date?
Какое сегодня число?
Ka-KO-jeh s'eh-VO-dn'a chis-LO?

What time does the shoe store open?
Во сколько открывается обувной магазин?
Va SKOL'-kə at-kry-VA-jeh-tsa a-buv-NOJ ma-ga-Z'IN?

Is today a holiday?
Сегодня праздник?
Se-VOD-n'a PRAZ-n'ik?

When is the next holiday?
Когда следующий праздник?
Kag-DA SL'EH-du-schij PRAZ-n'ik?

I will meet you at noon.
Встретимся в полдень.
FSTR'EH-t'im-s'a f POL-d'ehn'.

I will meet you later tonight.
Встретимся попозже вечером.
FSTR'EH-t'im-s'a pa-PO-zzheh V'EH-ch'eh-rəm.

My appointment is in ten minutes.

Моя встреча через десять минут.

Ma-JA FSTR'EH-cha CH'EH-r'ehz D'EH-s'at' m'i-NUT.

Can we meet in half an hour?

Мы можем встретиться через полчаса?

My MO-zhehm FSTR'EH-t'i-tsa CH'EH-r'ehz pol-cha-SA?

I will see you in March.

Увидимся в марте.

U-V'I-d'im-s'a v MAR-t'eh.

The meeting is scheduled for the twelfth.

Встреча назначена на двенадцатое число.

FSTR'EH-cha naz-NA-ch'eh-na na dv'eh-NA-tsa-tə-jeh ch'is-LO.

Can we set up the meeting for noon tomorrow?

Мы можем назначить встречу на завтра в полдень?

My MO-zhehm naz-NA-ch'it' FSTR'EH-chu na ZAF-tra f POL-d'ehn'?

What time will the cab arrive?

Во сколько приедет такси?

Va SKOL'-kə pr'i-JEH-d'eht tak-S'I?

Can you be here by midnight?

Ты сможешь быть здесь к полуночи?

Ty SMO-zhehsh byt' zd'ehs' k pa-LU-nə-chi?

The grand opening is scheduled for three o'clock.

Торжественное открытие назначено на три часа.

Tar-ZHEH-stv'ehn-nəjeh at-KRY-t'i-jeh naz-NA-ch'eh-nə na tr'i cha-SA.

When is your birthday?

Когда твой день рождения?

Kag-DA tvoj d'ehn' razh-D'EHN'-ja?

My birthday is on the second of June.

Мой день рождения второго июня.

Moj d'ehn' razh-D'EHN'-ja fta-RO-və i-JU-n'a.

This place opens at ten a.m.

Это место открывается в десять утра.

EH-tə M'EHS-tə at-kry-VA-jeh-tsa v D'EH-s'at' ut-RA.

From what time?

С которого часа?

S ka-TO-rə-və CHA-sa?

Sorry, it is already too late at night.

Извините, уже очень поздний вечер.

Iz-v'i-N'I-t'eh, u-ZHEH O-ch'ehn' POZ-n'ij V'EH-ch'ehr.

COMMON QUESTIONS

Do you speak English?
Вы говорите по-английски?
Vy ga-va-R'I-t'eh pa an-GL'IS-k'i?

What is your hobby?
Какое у вас хобби?
Ka-KO-jeh u vas HO-b'i?

What language do you speak?
На каком языке вы говорите?
Na ka-KOM jə-zy-K'EH vy ga-va-R'I-t'eh?

Was it hard?
Это было трудно?
EH-tə BY-lə TRUD-nə?

Can you help me?
Вы можете мне помочь?
Vy MO-zheh-t'eh mn'eh pa-MOCH?

Where can I find help?
Куда я могу обратиться за помощью?
Ku-DA ja ma-GU ab-ra-T'I-tsa za PO-ma-schju?

Where are we right now?
Где мы сейчас находимся?
Gd'eh my s'eh-CHAS na-HO-d'im-s'a?

Where were you last night?
Где ты был/была вчера вечером?
Gd'eh ty byl/by-LA vch'eh-RA V'Eh-ch'eh-rəm?

What type of a tree is that?
Что это за дерево?
Shto EH-tə za D'EH-r'eh-və?

Do you plan on coming back here again?
Вы планируете вернуться сюда снова?
Vy pla-N'I-ru-j'eh-t'eh ver-NU-tsja syu-DA SNO-va?

What kind of an animal is that?
Что это за животное?
Shto EH-tə za zhy-VOT-na-jeh?

Is that animal dangerous?
Это животное опасное?
EH-tə zhy-VOT-na-je a-PAS-nə-jeh?

Is it available?
Здесь свободно?
Zd'ehs' sva-BO-dnə?

Can we come see it?
Можно нам прийти посмотреть?
MOZH-nə nam pr'i-T'I pas-mat-R'EHT'?

Where do you live?
Где вы живёте?
Gd'eh vy zhy-V'O-t'eh?

Earl, what city are you from?
Эрл, из какого ты города?
Ehrl, is ka-KO-və ty GO-ra-da?

Is it a very large city?
Это очень большой город?
EH-tə O-ch'ehn' bal'-SHOJ GO-rəd?

Is there another available bathroom?
Есть ещё одна свободная уборная?
Jehst' jeh-SCH'O ad-NA sva-BO-dna-ja u-BOR-na-ja?

How was your trip?
Как прошла твоя поездка?
Kak prash-LA tva-JA pa-JEHZ-tka?

Is the bathroom free?
Уборная свободна?
U-BOR-na-ja sva-BOD-na?

How are you feeling?
Как ты себя чувствуешь?
Kak ty s'eh-B'A CHUS-tvu-jehsh?

Do you have any recommendations?
У вас есть какие-нибудь рекомендации?
U vas jehst' ka-K'I-jeh-n'i-but' r'eh-ka-m'ehn-DA-tsy-i?

When did you first come to China?
Когда вы впервые были в Китае?
Kag-DA vy fp'ehr-VY-jeh BY-l'i f k'i-TA-jeh?

Were you born here?
Ты родился/родилась здесь?
Ty ra-D'IL-s'a/ra-d'i-LAS' zd'ehs'?

Come join me for the rest of the vacation.
Приезжай ко мне, вместе проведём остаток отпуска.
Pr'i-jeh-ZZHAJ kə mn'eh, VM'EHS-t'eh pra-v'eh-D'OM as-TA-tək OT-pus-ka.

What time do the shops open in this area?
Во сколько в этом районе открываются магазины?
Va SKOL'-kə v EH-təm ra-JO-n'eh at-kry-VA-ju-tsa ma-ga-ZI-ny?

Is there tax-free shopping available?
Здесь есть магазины беспошлинной торговли?
Zd'ehs' jehst' ma-ga-Z'I-ny b'ehs-PO-shl'i-nəj tar-GOV-l'i?

Where can I change currency?
Где можно поменять деньги?
Gd'eh MO-zhnə pa-m'eh-N'AT' D'EHN'-g'i?

Is it legal to drink in this area?
Здесь разрешено пить?
Zd'ehs' raz-r'eh-sheh-NO p'it'?

Can I smoke in this area?
Здесь можно курить?
Zd'ehs' MO-zhnə ku-R'IT'?

What about this?
Как насчёт этого?
Kak nas-CH'OT EH-tə-və?

Can I park here?
Здесь можно парковаться?
Zd'ehs' MO-zhnə par-ka-VA-tsa?

Have you gotten used to living in Spain by now?
Ты уже привык/привыкла жить в Испании?
Ty u-ZHEH pr'i-VYK/pr'i-VYK-la zhyt' v is-PA-n'i-i?

How much does it cost to park here?
Сколько стоит припарковаться здесь?
SKOL'kə STO-it pr'i-par-ka-VA-tsa zd'ehs'?

How long can I park here?
На сколько я могу припарковаться здесь?
Na SKOL'-kə ja ma-GU pr'i-par-ka-VA-tsa zd'ehs'?

Where can I get some directions?
Где я могу узнать дорогу?
Gd'eh ja ma-GU uz-NAT' da-RO-gu?

Can you point me in the direction of the bridge?
Вы не могли бы указать мне дорогу к мосту?
Vy n'eh mag-L'I by u-ka-ZAT' mn'eh da-RO-gu k mas-TU?

What can I do here for fun?
Какие здесь есть развлечения?
Ka-K'I-jeh zd'ehs' jehst' raz-vl'eh-CH'EH-n'i-ja?

Is this a family-friendly place?
Это место подойдёт для семьи?
EH-tə M'EHS-tə pa-daj-D'OT dl'a s'ehm'-JI?

Are kids allowed here?
Сюда можно приходить с детьми?
S'u-DA MO-zhnə pr'i-ha-D'IT' z d'eht'-M'I?

Where can I find the park?
Где я могу найти парк?
Gd'eh ja ma-GU naj-T'I park?

How do I get back to my hotel?
Как мне вернуться в отель?
Kak mn'eh v'ehr-NU-tsa v a-TEHL'?

Where can I get some medicine?

Где можно купить лекарства?

Gd'eh MO-zhnə ku-P'IT' l'eh-KAR-stva?

Is my passport safe here?

Мой паспорт здесь в безопасности?

Moj PAS-pərt zd'ehs' v b'eh-za-PAS-nəs-t'i?

Do you have a safe for my passport and belongings?

У вас есть сейф для моего паспорта и личных вещей?

U vas jehst' s'ehjf dl'a ma-jeh-VO PAS-par-ta i 'LICH-nyh v'eh-SCHEHJ?

Is it safe to be here past midnight?

Здесь безопасно быть после полуночи?

Zd'ehs' b'eh-za-PAS-nə byt' POS-l'eh pa-LU-nə-chi?

When is the best time to visit this shop?

Когда лучше всего посетить этот магазин?

Kag-DA LU-chsheh fs'eh-VO pa-s'eh-T'IT' EH-tət ma-ga-Z'IN?

What is the best hotel in the area?

Какой лучший отель в этом районе?

Ka-KOJ LU-chshyj a-TEHL' v EH-təm ra-JO-n'eh?

What attractions are close to my hotel?

Какие достопримечательности есть рядом с моим отелем?

Ka-K'I-jeh das-ta-pr'i-m'eh-CHA-t'ehl'-nas-t'i jehst' R'A-dəm s ma-IM a-TEH-l'ehm?

Do you have any advice for tourists?

Вы можете что-нибудь посоветовать для туристов?

Vy MO-zheh-t'eh SHTO-n'i-but' pa-sa-V'EH-tə-vət' dl'a tu-RIS-təf?

Do you have a list of the top things to do in the area?

У вас есть список самых главных вещей, которые стоит сделать в этой местности?

U vas jehst' SPI-sək SA-myh GLAV-nyh v'eh-SCHEHJ, ka-TO-ry-jeh STO-it ZD'EH-lat' v EH-təj M'EHS-nas-t'i?

What do I need to pack to go there?

Что мне нужно взять с собой, чтобы пойти туда?

Shto mn'eh NU-zhnə vz'at' s sa-BOJ, SHTO-by paj-TI tu-DA?

Can you recommend me some good food to eat?
Вы можете посоветовать мне какую-нибудь хорошую еду?
Vy MO-zh'eh-t'eh pa-sa-V'EH-tə-vət' mn'eh ka-KU-ju-n'i-but' ha-RO-shu-ju jeh-DU?

What should I do with my time here?
Как я могу провести здесь время?
Kak ja ma-GU pra-v'ehs-T'I zd'ehs' VR'EH-m'a?

What is the cheapest way to get from my hotel to the shop?
Как дешевле всего добраться от отеля до магазина?
Kak d'eh-SHEHV-l'eh fs'eh-VO dab-RA-tsa at a-TEh-l'ya da ma-ga-Z'I-na?

What do you think of my itinerary?
Что вы думаете о моём маршруте?
Shto vy DU-ma-jeh-t'eh a ma-JOM mar-SHRU-t'eh?

Does my phone work in this country?
Мой телефон работает в этой стране?
Moj t'eh-l'eh-FON ra-BO-ta-jeht v EH-təj stra-N'EH?

What is the best route to get to my hotel?
По какой дороге лучше всего добраться до отеля?
Pa ka-KOJ da-RO-g'eh LU-chsheh fs'eh-VO dab-RA-tsa da a-TEh-l'a?

Will the weather be okay for outside activities?
Погода подойдёт для активного отдыха?
Pa-GO-da pa-daj-D'OT dl'a ak-T'IV-nə-və OD-dy-ha?

Was that rude?
Это было грубо?
EH-tə BY-lə GRU-bə?

Where should I stay away from?
Каких мест мне следует избегать?
Ka-K'IH m'hest mn'eh SL'EH-du-jeht iz-b'eh-GAT'?

What is the best dive site in the area?
Какое здесь лучшее место для дайвинга?
Ka-KO-jeh zd'ehs' LU-chsheh-jeh M'EHS-tə dl'a DAJ-v'in-ga?

What is the best beach in the area?
Какой здесь лучший пляж?
Ka-KOJ zd'ehs' LU-chshyj pl'azh?

Do I need reservations?
Мне нужно делать заказ заранее?
Mn'eh NU-zhnə D'EH-lat' za-KAZ za-RA-n'eh-jeh?

I need directions to the best local food.
Мне нужны рекомендации по лучшим местным блюдам.
Mn'eh nuzh-NY r'eh-ka-m'ehn-DA-tsy-i pa LU-chshym M'EH-snym BL'U-dəm.

What's your name?
Как вас зовут?
Kak vas za-VUT?

Where is the nearest place to eat?
Где ближайшее место, где можно поесть?
Gd'eh b'li-ZHAJ-sheh-jeh M'EHS-tə, gd'eh MO-zhnə pa-JEHST'?

Where is the nearest hotel?
Где находится ближайший отель?
Gd'eh na-HO-d'i-tsa bl'i-ZHAJ-shyj a-TEHL'?

Where is transportation?
Где ходит транспорт?
Gd'eh HO-d'it TRANS-pərt?

How much is this?
Сколько это стоит?
SKOL'-kə EH-tə STO-it?

Do you pay tax here?
Вы платите налог?
Vy PLA-t'i-t'eh na-LOG?

What types of payment are accepted?
Какие способы оплаты вы принимаете?
Ka-K'I-jeh SPO-sə-by ap-LA-ty vy pr'i-n'i-MA-jeh-t'eh?

Can you help me read this?
Вы не могли бы мне помочь прочитать это?
Vy n'eh mag-L'I by mn'eh pa-MOCH pra-ch'i-TAT' EH-tə?

What languages do you speak?
На каких языках вы говорите?
Na ka-K'IH jə-zy-KAH vy ga-va-R'I-t'eh?

Is it difficult to speak English?
Трудно ли говорить на английском?
TRU-dnə l'i ga-va-R'IT' na an-GL'I-skəm?

What does that mean?
Что это значит?
Shto EH-tə ZNA-ch'it?

What is your name?
Как вас зовут?
Kak vas za-VUT?

Do you have a lighter?
У вас есть зажигалка?
U vas jehst' za-zhy-GAL-ka?

Do you have a match?
У вас есть спички?
U vas jehst' SP'I-chk'i?

Is this a souvenir from your country?
Это сувенир из вашей страны?
EH-tə su-v'eh-N'IR iz VA-shehj stra-NY?

What is this?
Что это?
Shto EH-tə?

Can I ask you a question?
Могу я задать вам вопрос?
Ma-GU ja za-DAT' vam vap-ROS?

Where is the safest place to store my travel information?
Какое самое безопасное место для хранения моих проездных документов?
Ka-KO-jeh SA-mə-jeh b'eh-za-PA-sna-jeh M'EHS-tə dl'a hra-N'EH-n'i-ja ma-IH pra-jehz-NYH da-ku-M'EHN-təf?

Will you come along with me?
Ты пойдёшь со мной?
Ty paj-D'OSH sa mnoj?

Is this your first time here?
Вы здесь впервые?

Vy zd'ehs' fp'ehr-VY-jeh?

What is your opinion on the matter?
Что вы думаете по этому поводу?
Shto vy DU-ma-jeh-t'eh pa EH-tə-mu PO-və-du?

Will this spoil if I leave it out too long?
Это испортится, если я оставлю его надолго без холодильника?
EH-tə is-POR-t'i-tsa JES-l'i ja as-TAV-l'u jeh-VO na-DOL-gə b'ehs ha-la-D'IL'-n'i ka?

What side of the sidewalk do I walk on?
По какой стороне тротуара мне идти?
Pa ka-KOJ sta-ra-N'EH tra-tu-A-ra mn'eh i-T'I?

What do those lights mean?
Что означают эти огни?
Shto az-na-CHA-jut EH-t'i ag-N'I?

Can I walk up these stairs?
Можно мне подняться по лестнице?
MOZH-nə mn'eh pad-N'A-tsa pa L'EH-sn'i-tseh?

Is that illegal here?
Это здесь незаконно?
EH-tə zd'ehs' n'eh-za-KO-nnə?

How much trouble would I get in if I did that?
Что мне будет, если я сделаю это?
Shto mn'eh BU-d'eht, JEHS-l'i ja ZD'EH-la-ju EH-tə?

Why don't we all go together?
Почему бы нам не пойти всем вместе?
Pa-ch'eh-MU by nam n'eh paj-TI fs'ehm VM'EhS-t'eh?

May I throw away waste here?
Можно ли выбросить сюда мусор?
MOZH-nə l'i VYB-rə-sit' s'u-DA MU-sər?

Where is the recycle bin?
Где мусорный бак?

Gd'eh MU-sər-nyj bak?

WHEN SOMEONE IS BEING RUDE

Please, close your mouth while chewing that.
Пожалуйста, не жуйте с открытым ртом.
Pa-ZHA-lə-stə n'eh ZHUJ-t'eh s at-KRY-tym rtom.

Don't ask me again, please.
Пожалуйста, не спрашивайте меня снова.
Pa-ZHA-ləs-ta, n'eh SPRA-shy-vaj-t'eh m'eh-N'A SNO-va.

I'm not paying for that.
Я не буду платить за это.
Ja n'eh BU-du pla-T'IT' za EH-tə.

Leave me alone or I am calling the authorities.
Оставьте меня в покое, или я вызову полицию.
As-TAV'-t'eh m'eh-N'A f pa-KO-jeh, I-l'i ja VY-zə-vu pa-L'I-tsy-ju.

Hurry up!
Поторопитесь!
Pa-ta-ra-P'I-t'ehs'!

Stop bothering me!
Отстаньте от меня!
At-STAN'-t'eh at m'eh-N'A!

Don't bother me, please!
Не мешайте мне, пожалуйста!
N'eh m'eh-SHAJ-t'eh mn'e, pa-ZHA-lə-stə!

Are you content?
Вы довольны?
Vy da-VOL'-ny?

I'm walking away, please don't follow me.
Я ухожу, пожалуйста, не идите за мной.
Ja u-ha-ZHY, pa-ZHA-lə-stə, n'eh i-D'I-t'eh za mnoj.

You stole my shoes and I would like them back.

Вы украли мою обувь, и я хочу, чтобы вы вернули её.

Vy uk-RA-l'i ma-JU O-buf', i ja ha-CHU, SHTO-by vy v'ehr-NU-l'I jeh-JO.

You have the wrong person.

Вы ошиблись, я не при чём.

Vy a-SH'IB-l'is', ja n'eh pr'i ch'om.

I think you are incorrect.

По-моему, вы ошибаетесь.

Pa-MO-jeh-mu, vy a-shy-BA-jeh-t'ehs'.

Stop waking me up!

Перестаньте меня будить!

P'eh-r'ehs-TAN'-t'eh m'eh-N'A bu-D'IT'!

You're talking too much.

Вы слишком много говорите.

Vy SL'I-shkəm MNO-gə ga-va-R'I-t'eh.

That hurts!

Больно!

BOL'-nə!

I need you to apologize.

Вы должны извиниться.

Vy dal-ZHNY iz-v'i-N'I-tsa.

Stay away from my children!

Держитесь подальше от моих детей!

D'ehr-ZHY-t'ehs' pa-DAL'-sheh at ma-IH d'eh-T'EHJ!

Don't touch me.

Не прикасайтесь ко мне.

N'eh pr'i-ka-SAJ-t'ehs' ka mn'eh.

I would appreciate it if you didn't take my seat.

Я был/была бы признателен/признательна, если бы вы осободили моё место.

Ja byl/by-LA by pr'iz-NA-t'eh-l'en/pr'iz-NA-t'ehl'-na, JEHS-l'i by vy as-va-ba-D'I-l'i ma-JO M'ES-tə.

You didn't tell me that.

Вы мне этого не говорили.

Vy mn'eh EH-tə-və n'eh ga-va-R'I-l'i.

You are price gouging me.
Вы завышаете мне цены.
Vy za-vy-SHA-jeh-t'eh mn'eh TSEH-ny.

Please be quiet, I am trying to listen.
Пожалуйста, не шумите, я пытаюсь слушать.
Pa-ZHA-ləs-tə, n'eh shu-M'I-t'eh, ja py-TA-jus' SLU-shat'.

Don't interrupt me while I am talking.
Не перебивайте меня.
N'eh p'eh-r'eh-b'i-VAJ-t'eh m'eh-N'A.

Don't sit on my car and stay away from it.
Не садитесь на мою машину и держитесь от неё подальше.
N'eh sa-D'I-t'ehs' na ma-JU ma-SHY-nu i d'ehr-ZHY-t'ehs' at n'eh-YO pa-DAL'-sheh.

Get out of my car.
Выходи из моей машины.
Vy-ha-D'I iz ma-JEHJ ma-SHY-ny.

Get away from me and leave me alone!
Убирайтесь и оставьте меня в покое!
U-b'i-RAJ-t'ehs' i as-TAV'-t'eh m'eh-N'A f pa-KO-jeh!

You're being rude.
Вы грубо себя ведёте.
Vy GRU-bə s'eh-B'A v'eh-D'O-t'eh.

Please don't curse around my children.
Пожалуйста, не ругайтесь перед моими детьми.
Pa-ZHA-ləs-tə, n'eh ru-GAJ-t'ehs' P'EH-r'ehd ma-I-m'i d'eht'-M'I.

Let go of me!
Отпустите меня!
At-pus-T'I-t'eh m'eh-N'A!

I'm not going to tell you again.
Я не буду повторять.
Ja n'eh BU-du paf-ta-R'AT'.

Don't yell at me.
Не кричите на меня.
N'eh k'ri-CHI-t'eh na m'eh-N'A.

Please lower your voice.

Пожалуйста, говорите тише.

Pa-ZHA-ləs-tə, ga-va-R'I-t'eh T'I-sheh.

What is the problem?

В чём проблема?

F ch'om prab-L'EH-ma?

I would appreciate if you didn't take pictures of me.

Я не хочу, чтобы вы меня фотографировали.

Ja n'eh ha-CHU, SHTO-by vy m'eh-N'A fa-ta-gra-F'I-rə-və-l'i.

I am very disappointed in the way you are behaving.

Я очень разочарован/разочарована вашим поведением.

Ja O-chehn' ra-za-cha-RO-vən/ ra-za-cha-RO-vəna VA-shym pa-v'eh-D'EH-n'i-jehm.

Watch where you are walking!

Смотри, куда идёшь!

Smat-R'I, ku-DA i-D'OSH!

He just bumped into me!

Он просто врезался в меня!

On PROS-tə VR'EH-zal-s'a v m'eh-N'A!

MEDICAL

I would like to set up an appointment with my doctor.
Я бы хотел/хотела записаться на приём к врачу.
Ja by ha-T'EHL/ha-T'EH-la za-p'i-SA-tsa na pr'i-JOM k vra-CHU.

I am a new patient and need to fill out forms.
Я новый пациент, и мне нужно заполнить бумаги.
Ja NO-vyj pa-tsy-EHNT, i mn'eh NU-zhnə za-POL-n'it' bu-MA-g'i.

I am allergic to certain medications.
У меня аллергия на некоторые лекарства.
U m'eh-N'A a-l'ehr-G'I-ja na N'EH-kə-tə-ry-jeh l'eh-KAR-stva.

That is where it hurts.
Вот здесь болит.
Vot zd'ehs' ba-L'IT.

I have had the flu for three weeks.
У меня грипп уже три недели.
U m'eh-N'A gr'ip u-ZHEH tr'i n'eh-D'EH-l'i.

It hurts when I walk on that foot.
Мне больно, когда я наступаю на эту ногу.
Mn'eh BOL'-nə, kag-DA ja nastu-PA-ju na EH-tu NO-gu.

When is my next appointment?
Когда у меня следующий приём?
Kag-DA u m'eh-N'A SL'EH-du-ju-schij pr'i-JOM?

Does my insurance cover this?
Моя страховка покрывает это?
Ma-JA stra-HOF-ka pak-ry-VA-jeht EH-tə?

Do you want to take a look at my throat?
Хотите осмотреть моё горло?
Ha-T'I-t'eh as-mat-R'EHT' ma-JO GOR-lə?

Do I need to fast before going there?

Мне идти туда натощак?

Mn'eh i-T'I tu-DA na-ta-SCH'AK?

Is there a generic version of this medicine?

Есть ли дженерик для этого лекарства?

Jehst' l'i dzheh-N'EH-r'ik dl'a EH-tə-və l'eh-KAR-stva?

I need to get back on dialysis.

Мне нужно вернуться на диализ.

Mn'eh NU-zhnə v'ehr-NU-tsa na d'i-A-l'iz.

My blood type is A.

Моя группа крови — A.

Ma-JA GRU-pa KRO-v'i — A.

I will be more than happy to donate blood.

Я с удовольствием сдам кровь.

Ja s uda-VOL'-stv'i-jehm zdam krof'.

I have been feeling dizzy.

У меня кружится голова.

U m'eh-N'A KRU-zhy-tsa ga-la-VA.

The condition is getting worse.

Состояние ухудшается.

Sas-ta-JA-n'i-jeh u-hud-SHA-jeht-sa.

The medicine has made the condition a little better, but it is still there.

Лекарство немного улучшило состояние, но болезнь ещё не прошла.

Le-KAR-stvə n'eh-MNO-ga u-LU-chshy-lə sas-ta-JA-n'i-jeh, no ba-L'EHZN' jeh-SCH'O n'eh prash-LA.

Is my initial health examination tomorrow?

Мой первый медицинский осмотр завтра?

Moj P'EHR-vyj m'eh-d'i-TSYN-skjy as-MOTR ZAF-tra?

I would like to switch doctors.

Я бы хотел/хотела сменить врача.

Ja by ha-T'EHL/ha-T'EH-la sm'eh-N'IT' vra-CHA.

Can you check my blood pressure?

Вы можете измерить мне давление?

Vy MO-zheh-t'eh iz-M'EH-r'it' mn'eh dav-L'EH-n'i-jeh?

I have a fever that won't go away.
У меня не сбивается температура.
U m'eh-N'A n'eh zb'i-VA-jeh-tsa t'ehm-p'eh-ra-TU-ra.

I think my arm is broken.
Кажется, у меня сломана рука.
KA-zheh-tsa, u m'eh-N'A SLO-ma-na ru-KA.

I think I have a concussion.
Кажется, у меня сотрясение мозга.
KA-zheh-tsa, u m'eh-N'A sa-tr'a-S'EH-n'i-jeh MOZ-ga.

My eyes refuse to focus.
Я не могу сфокусировать взгляд.
Ja n'eh ma-GU sfa-ku-S'I-rə-vət' vzgl'at.

I have double vision.
У меня двоится в глазах.
U m'eh-N'A dva-I-tsa v gla-ZAH.

Is surgery the only way to fix this?
Операция — это единственный выход?
A-p'eh-RA-tsy-ja — EH-tə jeh-D'IN-stv'eh-nyj VY-həd?

Who are you referring me to?
К кому вы меня направляете?
K ka-MU vy m'eh-N'A nap-rav-L'A-jeh-t'eh?

Where is the waiting room?
Где находится приёмная?
Gd'eh na-HO-d'it-sa pr'i-JOM-na-ja?

Can I bring someone with me into the office?
Могу я взять кого-нибудь с собой в кабинет?
Ma-GU ja vz'at' ka-VO-n'i-but' s sa-BOJ f ka-b'i-N'EHT?

I need help filling out these forms.
Мне нужна помощь в заполнении этих бланков.
Mn'eh nuzh-NA PO-məsch v za-pal-N'EH-n'i-i EH-t'ih BLAN-kəf.

Do you take Cobra as an insurance provider?
Вы принимаете страхование COBRA?
Vy pr'i-n'i-MA-jeh-t'eh stra-ha-VA-n'i-jeh KOB-ra?

What is my copayment?

Какая моя совместная плата?

Ka-KA-ja ma-JA sav-M'EHS-na-ja PLA-ta?

What forms of payment do you accept?

Какие способы оплаты вы принимаете?

Ka-K'I-jeh SPO-sə-by ap-LA-ty vy pr'i-n'i-MA-j'eh-t'eh?

Do you have a payment plan, or is it all due now?

У вас есть план оплаты, или надо всё оплатить прямо сейчас?

U vas jehst' plan ap-LA-ty, I-l'i NA-də fs'o ap-la-T'IT' PR'A-mə se-CHAS?

My old doctor prescribed something different.

Мой предыдущий врач прописал мне другое лечение.

Moj pre-dy-DU-schij vrach pra-p'i-SAL mn'eh dru-GO-jeh l'eh-CH'EH-n'i-jeh.

Will you take a look at my leg?

Можете взглянуть на мою ногу?

MO-zheh-t'eh vzgl'a-NUT' na ma-JU NO-gu?

I need to be referred to a gynecologist.

Мне нужно направление к гинекологу.

Mn'eh NU-zhnnə nap-rav-L'EH-n'i-jeh k g'i-n'eh-KO-lə-gu.

I am unhappy with the medicine you prescribed me.

Мне не нравится лекарство, которое вы мне прописали.

Mn'eh n'eh NRA-v'it-sya l'eh-KAR-stvə, ka-TO-rə-jeh vy mn'eh pra-p'i-SA-l'i.

Do you see patients on the weekend?

Вы принимаете по выходным?

Vy pr'i-n'i-MA-j'eh-t'eh pa vy-had-NYM?

I need a good therapist.

Мне нужен хороший терапевт.

Mn'eh NU-zhehn ha-RO-shyj t'eh-ra-P'EHFT.

How long will it take me to rehab this injury?

Сколько мне понадобится времени, чтобы восстановиться после этой травмы?

SKOL'-kə mn'eh pa-NA-də-b'i-tsa VR'EH-m'eh-n'i, SHTO-by vas-ta-na-V'I-tsa POS-l'eh EH-təj TRAV-my?

I have not gone to the bathroom in over a week.

Я не испражнялся/испражнялась больше недели.

Ja n'eh is-prazh-N'AL-s'a/is-prazh-N'A-las' BOL'-sheh n'eh-D'EH-l'i.

I am constipated and feel bloated.

У меня запор и вздутие.

U m'eh-N'A za-POR i VZDU-t'i-jeh.

It hurts when I go to the bathroom.

Мне больно ходить в туалет.

Mn'eh BOL'-nə ha-D'IT' f tu-a-L'EHT.

I have not slept well at all since getting here.

Я плохо сплю с тех пор, как приехал/приехала сюда.

Ja PLO-hə spl'u s t'ehh por kak pr'i-JEH-hal/pr'i-JEH-ha-la s'u-DA.

Do you have any pain killers?

У вас есть обезболивающие?

U vas jehst' a-b'ehz-BO-l'eh-va-ju-sch'i-i?

I am allergic to that medicine.

У меня аллергия на это лекарство.

U m'eh-N'A a-l'ehr-G'I-ja na EH-tə l'eh-KAR-stvə.

How long will I be under observation?

Как долго меня будут наблюдать?

Kak DOL-gə m'eh-N'A BU-dut nab-l'u-DAT'?

I have a toothache.

У меня болит зуб.

U m'eh-N'A ba-L'IT zup.

Do I need to see a dentist?

Мне нужно сходить к стоматологу?

Mn'eh NU-zhnə s-ha-D'IT' k sta-ma-TO-lə-gu?

Does my insurance cover dental?

Моя страховка покрывает услуги стоматолога?

Ma-JA stra-HOF-ka pak-ry-VA-jeht us-LU-g'i sta-ma-TO-lə-gə?

My diarrhea won't go away.

У меня не проходит диарея.

U m'eh-N'A n'eh pra-HO-d'it d'i-a-R'EH-ja.

Can I have a copy of the receipt for my insurance?
Могу я получить копию квитанции для моей страховки?
Ma-GU ja pa-lu-CHIT' KO-p'i-ju kv'i-TAN-tsy-i dl'a ma-JEHJ stra-HOF-k'i?

I need a pregnancy test.
Мне нужен тест на беременность.
Mn'eh NU-zhehn tehst na b'eh-R'EH-m'eh-nəst'.

I think I may be pregnant.
Кажется, я беременна.
KA-zheh-tsa ja b'eh-R'EH-m'eh-nə.

Can we please see a pediatrician?
Можно нам обратиться к педиатру?
MOZH-nə nam ab-ra-T'I-tsa k p'eh-d'i-A-tru?

I have had troubles breathing.
Мне трудно дышать.
Mn'eh TRUD-nə DY-shat'.

My sinuses are acting up.
Меня беспокоят мои пазухи.
M'eh-N'A b'ehs-pa-KO-jat ma-I PA-zu-h'i.

Will I still be able to breastfeed?
Мне можно будет кормить грудью?
Mn'eh MO-zhnə BU-d'eht kar-M'IT' GRUD'-ju?

How long do I have to stay in bed?
Сколько мне нужно соблюдать постельный режим?
SKOL'-kə mn'eh NU-zhnə sab-l'u-DAT' past-T'EHL'-nyj r'eh-ZHYM?

How long do I have to stay under hospital care?
Сколько я буду лежать в больнице?
SKOL'-kə ja BU-du l'eh-ZHAT' v bal'-N'I-tseh?

Is it contagious?
Это заразно?
EH-tə za-RAZ-nə?

How far along am I?
На каком я месяце?
Na ka-KOM ja M'EH-s'a-tseh?

What did the x-ray say?
Что показал рентген?
Shto pa-ka-ZAL r'ehn-G'EHN?

Can I walk without a cane?
Я могу ходить без трости?
Ja ma-GU ha-D'IT' b'ehs TROS-t'i?

Is the wheelchair necessary?
Инвалидная коляска необходима?
In-va-L'ID-na-ja ka-L'AS-ka n'eh-ab-ha-D'I-ma?

Am I in the right area of the hospital?
Я в нужном отделении больницы?
Ja v NU-zhnəm at-d'eh-L'EH-n'i-i bal'-N'I-tsy?

Where is the front desk receptionist?
Где находится регистратура?
Gd'eh na-HO-d'i-tsa r'eh-g'is-tra-TU-ra?

I would like to go to a different waiting area.
Я бы хотел/хотела пойти в другую приёмную.
Ja by ha-T'EHL/ha-T'EH-la paj-T'I v dru-GU-ju pr'i-JOM-nə-ju.

Can I have a change of sheets, please?
Не могли бы вы сменить мне постельное бельё?
N'eh mag-L'I by vy sm'eh-N'IT' mn'eh pas-t'ehl'-na-jeh b'ehl'-JO?

Excuse me, what is your name?
Простите, как вас зовут?
Pras-T'I-t'eh, kak vas za-VUT?

Who is the doctor in charge here?
Кто здесь главный врач?
Kto zd'ehs' GLAV-nyj vrach?

I need some assistance, please.
Мне нужна помощь, пожалуйста.
Mn'eh nuzh-NA PO-məsch, pa-ZHA-ləs-tə.

Will my recovery affect my ability to do work?
Моя реабилитация повлияет на мою способность работать?
Ma-JA re-a-b'i-l'i-TA-tsy-ja pav-l'i-JA-jeht na ma-JU spa-SOB-nəst' ra-BO-tat'?

How long is the estimated recovery time?

Сколько примерно займёт выздоровление?

SKOL'kə pr'i-M'EHR-nə zaj-M'OT vyz-da-rav-L'EH-n'i-jeh?

Is that all you can do for me? There has to be another option.

Это всё, что вы можете для меня сделать? Должен быть другой вариант.

EH-tə fs'o, shto vy MO-zheh-t'eh dl'a m'eh-N'A ZD'EH-lat'? DOL-zhehn byt' dru-GOJ va-r'i-ANT.

I need help with motion sickness.

Мне нужно средство от укачивания.

Mn'eh NUZH-nə SR'EH-tstvə at u-KA-chi-va-n'i-ja.

I'm afraid of needles.

Я боюсь иголок.

Ja ba-JUS' i-GO-lək.

My gown is too small; I need another one.

Моя сорочка слишком мала, мне нужна другая.

Ma-JA sa-ROCH-ka SL'ISH-kəm ma-LA, mn'eh nuzh-NA dru-GA-ja.

Can I have extra pillows?

Можно мне ещё подушек?

MOZH-nə mn'eh jeh-SCH'O pa-DU-shək?

I need assistance getting to the bathroom.

Мне нужна помощь, чтобы сходить в туалет.

Mn'eh nuzh-NA PO-məsch, SHTO-by sha-D'IT' f tua-l'EHT.

Hi, is the doctor in?

Здравствуйте, доктор на месте?

ZDRA-stvuj-t'eh, DO-ktər na M'EHST-t'eh?

When should I schedule the next checkup?

Когда мне запланировать следующий осмотр?

Kag-DA mn'eh zap-la-N'I-rə-vət' SL'EH-du-ju-schij as-MOTR?

When can I have these stitches removed?

Когда мне снимут швы?

Kag-DA mn'eh SN'I-mut shvy?

Do you have any special instructions while I'm in this condition?

У вас какие-нибудь особые рекомендации для такого состояния?

U vas jehst' ka-K'I-jeh-n'i-but' a-SO-by-jeh r'eh-ka-m'ehn-DA-tsy-i dl'a ta-KO-və sas-ta-JA-n'i-ja?

ORDERING FOOD

Can I see the menu?
Можно посмотреть меню?
MOZH-nə pas-mat-R'EHT' m'eh-N'U?

I'm really hungry. We should eat something soon.
Я очень голоден/голодна. Скоро надо будет поесть.
Ja O-chehn' GO-lə-d'ehn/ga-la-DNA. SKO-rə NA-də BU-d'eht pa-JEHST'.

Can I take a look in the kitchen?
Могу я заглянуть на кухню?
Ma-GU ja zag-l'a-NUT' na KUH-n'u?

Can we see the drink menu?
Можно нам карту напитков?
MOZH-nə nam KAR-tu na-P'IT-kəf?

Where can we be seated?
Куда нам можно сесть?
Ku-DA nam MOZH-nə s'ehst'?

This is very tender and delicious.
Очень нежно и вкусно.
O-chehn' N'EHZH-nə i FKUS-nə.

Do you serve alcohol?
Вы подаёте алкоголь?
Vy pa-da-JO-t'eh al-ka-GOL'?

I'm afraid our party can't make it.
Боюсь, мы не сможем к вам присоединиться.
Ba-JUS', my neh SMO-zehm k vam pr'i-so'-jeh-d'i-N'I-tsa.

That room is reserved for us.
Это место зарезервировано для нас.
EH-tə M'EHS-tə za-r'eh-z'ehr-V'I-rə-və-nə dl'a nas.

Are there any seasonal favorites that you serve?
Вы подаёте какие-нибудь популярные сезонные блюда?
Vy pa-da-YO-t'eh ka-K'I-jeh-n'i-but' pa-pu-L'AR-ny-jeh s'eh-ZON-ny-jeh BL'U-da?

Do you offer discounts for kids or seniors?
У вас есть скидки для детей или пенсионеров?
U vas jehst' SK'IT-k'i dl'a d'eh-T'EHJ I-l'i p'ehn-s'i-a-N'EH-rəf?

I would like it filleted.
Я бы хотел/хотела это в виде филе.
Ja by ha-T'EHL/ha-T'EH-la EH-tə v V'I-d'eh f'i-L'EH.

I would like to reserve a table for a party of four.
Я бы хотел/хотела заказать столик для четырёх человек.
Ja by ha-T'EHL/ha-T'EH-la za-ka-zat' STO-lik dl'a ch'eh-ty-R'OCH ch'eh-la-V'EHK.

I would like to place the reservation under my name.
Я бы хотел/хотела сделать заказ на своё имя.
Ja by ha-T'EHL/ha-T'EH-la ZD'EH-lat' za-KAZ na sva-JO I-m'a.

What type of alcohol do you serve?
Какой алгоколь вы подаёте?
Ka-KOJ al-ka-GOL' vy pa-da-JO-t'eh?

Do I need a reservation?
Мне нужно делать заказ заранее?
Mn'eh NU-zhnə D'EH-lat' za-KAZ za-RA-n'eh-jeh?

What does it come with?
С чем это подают?
S ch'ehm EH-tə pa-da-JUT?

What are the ingredients?
Какие здесь ингредиенты?

Ka-K'I-jeh zd'ehs' in-gr'eh-d'i-JEHN-ty?

What else does the chef put in the dish?
Что ещё шеф-повар кладёт в блюдо?
Shto jeh-SCH'O shehf-PO-var kla-D'OT v BL'U-də?

I wonder which of these tastes better?

А что из этого вкуснее?

A shto iz EH-tə-və fkus-N'EH-jeh?

That is incorrect. Our reservation was at noon.

Это ошибка. Наша бронь была на полдень.

EH-tə a-SHYB-ka. NA-sha bron' by-LA na POL-d'ehn'.

I would like red wine, please.

Я буду красное вино, пожалуйста.

Ja BU-du KRAS-na-jeh v'i-NO, pa-ZHA-ləs-tə.

Can you choose the soup?

Вы можете выбрать суп?

Vy MO-zheh-t'eh VYB-rat' sup?

What is the most popular dish here?

Какое здесь самое популярное блюдо?

Ka-KO-jeh zd'ehs' SA-mə-jeh pa-pu-L'AR-na-jeh BL'U-də?

What are the specials today?

Какие сегодня блюда дня?

Ka-K'I-jeh s'eh-VO-dn'a BL'U-də dn'a?

What are your appetizers?

Какие у вас закуски?

Ka-K'I-jeh u vas za-KUS-k'i?

Please bring these out separately.

Пожалуйста, подайте это по отдельности.

Pa-ZHA-ləs-tə, pa-DAJ-t'eh EH-tə pə at-D'EHL'-nas-t'i.

Do we leave a tip?

Оставим чаевые?

As-TA-v'im tcha-jeh-VY-jeh?

Are tips included with the bill?

Чаевые включены в счёт?

Tcha-jeh-VY-jeh fkl'u-cheh-NY f sch'ot?

Split the bill, please.

Пожалуйста, принесите раздельный счёт.

Pa-ZHA-ləs-tə, pr'i-n'eh-S'I-t'ey raz-D'EHL'-nyj sch'ot.

We are paying separately.

Мы будем платить по отдельности.

My BU-d'ehm pla-t'it' pa əd-D'EHL'-nas-t'i.

Is there an extra fee for sharing an entrée?

Нужно ли платить дополнительно, если мы хотим разделить основное блюдо?

NUZH-nə l'i pla-T'IT' da-pal-N'I-t'ehl-nə, JEHS-l'i my ha-T'IM raz-d'eh-L'IT' as-nav-NO-jeh BL'U-də?

Is there a local specialty that you recommend?

Есть ли какое-нибудь особое местное блюдо, которое вы можете порекомендовать?

Jehst' l'i ka-KO-jeh-n'i-but' M'EHS-nə-jeh BL'U-də, ka-TO-rə-jeh vy MO-zheh-t'eh pa-r'eh-ka-m'ehn-da-VAT'?

This looks different from what I originally ordered.

Это не похоже на то, что я заказал/заказала.

EH-tə n'eh pa-HO-zheh na to, shto ja za-ka-ZAL/za-ka-ZA-la.

Is this a self-serve buffet?

Это «шведский стол»?

EH-tə SHV'EHT-skij stol?

I want a different waiter.

Мне нужен другой официант.

Mn'eh NU-zhehn dru-GOJ a-f'i-tsy-ANT.

Please move us to a different table.

Пожалуйста, пересадите нас за другой столик.

Pa-ZHA-ləs-tə, p'eh-r'eh-sa-D'I-t'eh nas za dru-GOJ STO-l'ik.

Can we put two tables together?

Мы можем поставить два столика вместе?

My MO-zhehm pas-TA-v'it' dva STO-l'i-ka VM'EHS-t'eh?

My spoon is dirty. Can I have another one?

Моя ложка грязная. Можно мне другую?

Ma-JA LO-zhka GR'A-zna-ja. MO-zhnə mn'eh dru-GU-ju?

We need more napkins, please.

Нам нужно ещё салфеток, пожалуйста.

Nam NU-zhnə jeh-SCH'O sal-F'EH-tək, pa-ZHA-ləs-tə.

I'm a vegetarian and don't eat meat.

Я вегетарианец/вегетарианка и не ем мясо.

Ja v'eh-g'eh-ta-r'i-A-n'ehts/ v'eh-g'eh-ta-r'i-A-nka i n'eh jehm M'A-sə.

The table next to us is being too loud. Can you say something?

За соседним столиком слишком шумно. Не могли бы вы сделать им замечание?

Za sa-S'HED-n'im STO-l'i-kəm SLISH-kəm SHUM-nə. N'eh mag-L'I by vy ZD'EH-lat' im za-m'eh-CHA-n'i-jeh?

Someone is smoking in our non-smoking section.

Кто-то курит в нашем зале для некурящих.

KTO-tə KU-r'it v NA-shehm ZA-l'he dl'a n'eh-ku-R'A-schih.

Please seat us in a booth.

Посадите нас в полукабинет, пожалуйста.

Pa-sa-D'I-t'eh nas f po-lu-ka-b'i-N'HET, pə-ZHA-ləs-tə.

Do you have any non-alcoholic beverages?

У вас есть безалкогольные напитки?

U vas jehst' b'ehz-al-ka-GOL'-ny-jeh na-P'IT-k'i?

Where is your bathroom?

Где у вас уборная?

Gd'eh u vas u-BOR-na-ja?

Are you ready to order?

Вы готовы сделать заказ?

Vy ga-TO-vy ZD'EH-lat' za-KAZ?

Five more minutes, please.

Ещё пять минут, пожалуйста.

Jeh-SCH'O p'at' m'i-NUT, pə-ZHA-ləs-tə.

What time do you close?

Во сколько вы закрываетесь?

Va SKOL'-kə vy zak-ry-VA-j'eh-t'ehs'?

Is there pork in this dish? I don't eat pork.

В этом блюде есть свинина? Я не ем свинину.

V EH-təm BL'U-d'eh jehst' sv'i-N'I-na? Ja n'eh jehm sv'i-N'I-nu.

Do you have any dishes for vegans?

У вас есть блюда для веганов?

U vas jehst' BL'U-da dl'a V'EH-gə-nəf?

Are these vegetables fresh?
Эти овощи свежие?
EH-t'i O-va-schi SV'EH-zhy-jeh?

Have any of these vegetables been cooked in butter?
Какие-нибудь из этих овощей готовили в сливочном масле?
Ka-K'I-jeh-n'i-but' iz EH-t'ih a-va-SCH'EHJ ga-TO-v'i-l'i f SL'I-va-chnəm MAS-l'eh?

Is this spicy?
Это блюдо острое?
EH-tə BL'U-də OS-trə-jeh?

Is this sweet?
Это сладкое?
EH-tə SLAT-kə-jeh?

I want more, please.
Я хочу ещё, пожалуйста.
Ja ha-CHU jeh-SCH'O, pa-ZHA-ləs-tə.

I would like a dish containing these items.
Я бы хотел/хотела блюдо с этими ингредиентами.
Ja by ha-T'EHL/ha-T'EH-la BL'U-də s EH-t'i-m'i in-gr'eh-d'i-JEHN-ta-m'i.

Can you make this dish light? Thank you.
Вы можете сделать это блюдо лёгким? Спасибо.
Vy MO-zheh-t'eh ZD'EH-lat' EH-tə BL'U-də L'OH-k'im? Spa-S'I-bə.

Nothing else.
Больше ничего.
BOL'-sheh n'i-ch'eh-VO.

Please clear the plates.
Пожалуйста, уберите тарелки.
Pa-ZHA-ləs-tə, u-b'eh-R'I-t'eh ta-R'EHL-k'i .

May I have a cup of soup?
Можно мне тарелку супа?
MOZH-nə mn'eh ta-R'EHL-ku SU-pa?

Do you have any bar snacks?
У вас есть закуски из бара?
U vas j'ehst' za-KUS-k'I iz BA-ra?

Another round, please.
Повторите напитки, пожалуйста.
Paf-ta-R'I-t'eh na-P'IT-k'i, pa-ZHA-ləs-tə.

When is closing time for the bar?
Во сколько закрывается бар?
Va SKOL'-kə zak-ry-VA-jeh-tsa bar?

That was delicious!
Это было очень вкусно!
EH-tə BY-lə O-ch'ehn' FKUS-nə!

Does this have alcohol in it?
Здесь есть алкоголь?
Zd'ehs' jehst' al-ka-GOL'?

Does this have nuts in it?
Здесь есть орехи?
Zd'ehs' jehst' a-R'EH-h'i?

Is this gluten free?
Это без глютена?
EH-tə b'ehz gl'u-T'EH-nə?

Can I get this to go?
Могу я взять это с собой?
Ma-GU ja vz'at' EH-tə s sa-BOJ?

May I have a refill?
Вы можете налить мне ещё?
Vy MO-zheh-t'eh na-L'IT' mn'eh jeh-SCH'O?

Is this dish kosher?
Это блюдо кошерное?
EH-tə BL'U-də ka-SHEHR-na-jeh?

I would like to change my drink.
Я бы хотел/хотела сменить напиток.
Ja by ha-T'EHL/ha-T'EH-la sm'eh-N'IT' na-P'I-tək.

My coffee is cold. Could you please warm it up?
Мой кофе холодный. Вы не могли бы подогреть его?
Moj KO-f'eh ha-LOD-nyj. Vy n'eh mag-L'I by pa-dag-R'EHT' jeh-VO?

Do you serve coffee?

Вы подаёте кофе?

Vy pa-da-JO-t'eh KO-f'eh?

Can I please have cream in my coffee?

Можно мне, пожалуйста, сливки в кофе?

MOZH-nə mn'eh, pa-ZHA-ləs-tə, SL'IF-k'i f KO-f'eh?

Please add extra sugar to my coffee.

Пожалуйста, положите дополнительный сахар в мой кофе.

Pa-ZHA-ləs-tə, pa-la-ZHY-t'eh da-pal-N'I-t'ehl'-nyj SA-har v moj KO-f'eh.

I would like to have my coffee served black, no cream and no sugar.

Я хочу чёрный кофе, без сливок и сахара.

Ja ha-CHU CH'OR-nyj KO-f'eh, b'ehs SL'I-vək i SA-ha-ra.

I would like to have decaffeinated coffee, please.

Я буду кофе без кофеина, пожалуйста.

Ja BU-du KO-f'eh b'ehs ka-f'eh-I-na, pa-ZHA-ləs-tə.

Do you serve coffee-flavored ice cream?

У вас есть мороженое с ароматом кофе?

U vas jehst' ma-RO-zheh-na-jeh s a-ra-MA-təm KO-f'eh?

Please put my cream and sugar on the side so that I can add it myself.

Пожалуйста, положите сливки и сахар на блюдце, чтобы я мог/могла добавить их сам/сама.

Pa-ZHA-ləs-tə, pa-la-ZHY-t'eh SL'IF-k'i i SA-har na BL'UD-tseh, SHTO-by ja mog/mag-LA da-BA-v'it' ih sam/sa-MA.

I would like to order an iced coffee.

Я бы хотел/хотела заказать кофе со льдом.

Ja by ha-T'EHL/ha-T'EH-la za-ka-ZAT' KO-f'eh sə l'dom.

I would like an espresso please.

Эспрессо, пожалуйста.

Ehs-PREH-sə, pa-ZHA-ləs-tə.

Do you have 2% milk?

У вас есть двухпроцентное молоко?

U vas jehst' dvuh-pra-TSEHN-tna-jeh ma-la-KO?

Do you serve soy milk?

У вас есть соевое молоко?

U vas jehst' SO-jeh-və-jeh ma-la-KO?

Do you have almond milk?

У вас есть миндальное молоко?

U vas jehst' m'in-DAL'-na-jeh ma-la-KO?

Are there any alternatives to the milk you serve?

У вас есть заменители молока?

U vas jehst' za-m'eh-N'I-t'eh-l'i ma-la-KA?

Please put the lemons for my tea on the side.

Пожалуйста, оставьте лимон для моего чая на блюдце.

Pa-ZHA-ləs-tə, as-TAV't'eh l'i-MON dl'a ma-jeh-VO CHA-ja na BL'UD-tseh.

No lemons with my tea, thank you.

Чай без лимона, спасибо.

Chaj b'ehz l'i-MO-na, spa-S'I-bə.

Is your water from the tap?

Ваша вода из-под крана?

VA-sha va-DA IS-pəd KRA-na?

Sparkling water, please.

Газированной воды, пожалуйста.

Ga-z'il-RO-va-nəj va-DY, pa-ZHA-ləs-tə.

Can I get a diet coke?

Можно мне диетическую колу?

MOZH-nə mn'eh d'i-jeh-T'I-ch'ehs-ku-ju KO-lu?

We're ready to order.

Мы готовы сделать заказ.

My ga-TO-vy ZD'EH-lat' za-KAS.

Can we be seated over there instead?

Можно нам лучше сесть туда?

MOZH-nə nam LU-chsheh s'ehst' tu-DA?

Can we have a seat outside?

Можно нам столик снаружи?

MOZH-nə nam STO-l'ik sna-RU-zhy?

Please don't add the salt.

Пожалуйста, не добавляйте соль.

Pa-ZHA-ləs-tə, n'eh da-bav-L'AJ-t'eh sol'.

This is what I would like for my main course.
Я буду это в качестве основного блюда.
Ja BU-du EH-tə f KA-chə-stv'ə as-nav-NO-və BL'U-də.

I would like the soup instead of the salad.
Я бы хотел/хотела суп вместо салата.
Ja by ha-T'EHL/ha-T'EH-la sup VM'EHS-tə sa-LA-ta.

I'll have the chicken risotto.
Я возьму ризотто с курицей.
Ja vaz'MU r'i-ZO-tə s KU-r'i-tsehj.

Can I change my order?
Могу я изменить свой заказ?
Ma-GU ja iz-m'eh-N'IT' svoj za-KAZ?

Do you have a kids' menu?
У вас есть детское меню?
U vas jehst' D'EHT-skə-jeh m'eh-N'U?

When does the lunch menu end?
Во сколько вы перестаёте подавать обеденное меню?
Va SKOL'-kə vy p'eh-r'eh-sta-JO-t'eh pa-da-VAT' a-B'EH-d'eh-na-jeh m'eh-N'U?

When does the dinner menu start?
Во сколько вы начинаете подавать меню ужина?
Va SKOL'-kə vy na-ch'i-NA-j'eh-t'eh pa-da-VAT' m'eh-N'U U-zhy-na?

Do you have any recommendations from the menu?
Вы можете посоветовать что-нибудь из меню?
Vy MO-zheh-t'eh pa-sa-V'EH-ta-vat' SHTO-n'i-but' iz m'eh-N'U?

I would like to place an off-menu order.
Я бы хотел/хотела заказать что-то, чего нет в меню.
Ja by ha-T'EHL/ha-T'EH-la za-ka-ZAT' SHTO-tə, ch'eh-VO n'eht v m'eh-N'U.

Can we see the dessert menu?
Можно нам десертную карту?
MOZH-nə nam d'eh-S'EHR-tnə-ju KAR-tu?

Is this available sugar-free?
У вас есть это без сахара?
U vas jehst' EH-tə b'ehs SA-ha-ra?

May we have the bill, please?

Можно нам счёт, пожалуйста?

MOZH-nə nam sch'ot, pa-ZHA-ləs-tə?

Where do we pay?

Где мы можем заплатить?

Gd'eh my MO-zhehm zap-la-T'IT'?

Hi, we are with the party of Isaac.

Здравствуйте, мы вместе с Исааком.

ZDRA-stvuj-t'eh, my VM'EHS-t'eh s Isa-A-kəm.

We haven't made up our minds yet on what to order. Can we have a few more minutes, please?

Мы ещё не решили, что заказать. Можете дать нам ещё пару минут, пожалуйста?

My jeh-SCH'O n'eh r'eh-SHY-l'i, shto za-ka-ZAT'. MO-zheh-t'eh dat' nam jeh-SCH'O PA-ru m'i-NUT, pa-ZHA-ləs-tə?

Waiter!

Официант!

A-f'i-tsy-ANT!

Waitress!

Официантка!

A-f'i-tsy-ANT-ka!

I'm still deciding, come back to me, please.

Я ещё не выбрал/выбрала, вы можете подойти попозже, пожалуйста?

Ja jeh-SCH'O n'eh VYB-ral/VYB-ra-la, vy MO-zheh-t'eh pa-daj-T'I pa-PO-ZZHEH, pa-ZHA-ləs-tə?

Can we have a pitcher of that?

Можно нам графин этого напитка?

MOZH-nə nam gra-F'IN EH-tə-və na-P'IT-ka?

This is someone else's meal.

Это не мой заказ.

EH-tə n'eh moj za-KAS.

Can you please heat this up a little more?

Не могли бы вы подогреть это ещё немного?

N'eh mag-L'I by vy pa-dag-R'EHT' EH-tə jeh-SCH'O n'ehm-NO-gə?

I'm afraid I didn't order this.
Боюсь, я этого не заказывал/заказывала.
Ba-JUS' ja EH-tə-və n'eh za-KA-zy-val/za-KA-zy-va-la.

The same thing again, please.
То же самое, пожалуйста.
To zheh SA-mə-jeh, pa-ZHA-ləs-tə.

Can we have another bottle of wine?
Можно нам ещё бутылку вина?
MOZH-nə nam jeh-SCH'O bu-TYL-ku v'i-NA?

That was perfect, thank you!
Это было прекрасно, спасибо!
EH-tə BY-lə pr'ehk-RAS-nə, spa-S'I-bə!

Everything was good.
Всё было очень хорошо.
Fs'o BY-lə O-ch'ehn' ha-ra-SHO.

Can we have the bill?
Можно нам счёт?
MOZH-nə nam sch'ot?

I'm sorry, but this bill is incorrect.
Извините, но этот счёт неверный.
Iz-v'i-N'I-t'eh, no EH-tət sch'ot n'eh-V'EHR-nyj.

Can I have clean cutlery?
Можно мне чистые приборы?
MOZH-nə mn'eh CHIS-ty-jeh pr'i-BO-ry?

Can we have more napkins?
Можете принести нам ещё салфеток?
MO-zheh-t'eh pr'i-n'ehs-T'I nam jeh-SCH'O sal-F'EH-tək?

May I have another straw?
Можно мне ещё одну соломинку?
MOZH-nə mn'eh jeh-SCH'O ad-NU sa-LO-m'in-ku?

What sides can I have with that?
Какой гарнир подойдёт к этому?
Ka-KOJ gar-N'IR pa-daj-D'OT k EH-tə-mu?

Excuse me, but this is overcooked.
Извините, но это блюдо передержали.
Iz-v'i-N'I-t'eh, no EH-tə BL'U-də p'eh-r'eh-d'ehr-ZHA-l'i.

May I talk to the chef?
Могу я поговорить с шеф-поваром?
Ma-GU ja pa-ga-va-R'IT' s shehf-PO-va-rəm?

We have booked a table for fifteen people.
Мы заказали столик на пятнадцать персон.
My za-ka-ZA-l'i STO-l'ik na p'at-NA-tsat' p'ehr-SON.

Are there any tables free?
Есть свободные столики?
Jehst' sva-BOD-ny-jeh STO-l'i-k'i?

I would like one beer, please.
Одно пиво, пожалуйста.
Ad-NO P'I-və, pa-ZHA-ləs-tə.

Can you add ice to this?
Вы можете добавить сюда льда?
Vy MO-zheh-t'eh da-BA-v'it' s'u-DA l'da?

I would like to order a dark beer.
Я бы хотел/хотела заказать тёмное пиво.
Ja by ha-T'EHL/ha-T'EH-la za-ka-ZAT' T'OM-nə-jeh P'I-və.

Do you have any beer from the tap?
У вас есть разливное пиво?
U vas jehst' raz-l'iv-NO-jeh PI-və?

How expensive is your champagne?
Сколько стоит ваше шампанское?
SKOL'-kə STO-it VA-sheh sham-PAN-skə-jeh?

Enjoy your meal.
Приятного аппетита!
Pr'i-YAT-nə-və ap'eh-T'I-ta!

I want this.
Я хочу это.
Ja ha-CHU EH-tə.

Please cook my meat well done.
Пожалуйста, прожарьте моё мясо полностью.
Pa-ZHA-ləs-tə, pra-ZHAR'-t'eh ma-JO M'A-sə POL-nəs-t'u.

Please cook my meat medium rare.
Пожалуйста, сделайте мне мясо средней прожарки.
Pa-ZHA-ləs-tə, ZD'EH-lahj-t'eh mn'eh M'A-sə SR'EHD-n'ehj pra-ZHAR-k'i.

Please prepare my meat rare.
Пожалуйста, приготовьте мне мясо с кровью.
Pa-ZHA-ləs-tə, pr'i-ga-TOF'-t'eh mn'eh M'A-sə s KRO-v'u.

What type of fish do you serve?
Какую рыбу вы подаёте?
Ka-KU-ju RY-bu vy pa-da-JO-t'eh?

Can I make a substitution with my meal?
Могу я заменить кое-что в моей еде?
MA-gu ja za-m'eh-N'IT' KO-jeh-SHTO v ma-JEHJ jeh-D'EH?

Do you have a booster seat for my child?
У вас есть детский стул для моего ребёнка?
U vas jehst' D'EHT-skij stul dl'a ma-jeh-VO r'eh-B'ON-ka?

Call us when you get a table.
Позовите нас, когда у вас появится столик.
Pa-za-V'I-t'eh nas, kag-DA u vas pa-JA-v'i-tsa STO-l'ik.

Is this a non-smoking section?
Это зал для некурящих?
EH-tə zal dl'a n'eh-ku-R'A-schih?

We would like to be seated in the smoking section.
Мы бы хотели столик в зале для курящих.
My by ha-T'EH-l'i STO-l'ik v ZA-l'eh dl'a ku-R'A-schih.

This meat tastes funny.
У этого мяса странный вкус.
U EH-tə-və M'A-sa STRAN-nyj fkus.

More people will be joining us later.
Позже к нам ещё присоединятся люди.
POZH-zheh k nam jeh-SCH'O pr'i-sa-jeh-d'i-N'A-tsa L'U-d'i.

TRANSPORTATION

Where's the train station?
Где находится железнодорожный вокзал?
Gd'eh na-HO-d'i-tsa zhe'l'ehzna-da-ROZH-nyj vak-ZAL?

How much does it cost to get to this address?
Сколько стоит поездка по этому адресу?
SKOL'-kə STO-it pa-JEH-stkə pa EH-tə-mu AD-r'eh-su?

What type of payment do you accept?
Какие способы оплаты вы принимаете?
Ka-K'I-jeh SPO-sə-by ap-LA-ty vy pr'i-n'i-MA-j'eh-t'eh?

Do you have first-class tickets available?
У вас есть билеты в первый класс?
U vas jehst' b'i-L'EH-ty f P'EHR-vyj klas?

What platform do I need to be on to catch this train?
На какую платформу прибывает этот поезд?
Na ka-KU-ju plat-FOR-mu pr'i-by-VA-jeht EH-tət PO-jehzd?

Are the roads paved in this area?
Дороги в этом районе асфальтированы?
Da-RO-g'i v EH-təm ra-JO-n'eh as-fal'-T'I-rə-və-ny?

Where are the dirt roads, and how do I avoid them?
Где грунтовые дороги, и как мне их избежать?
Gd'eh grun-TO-vy-jeh da-RO-g'i i kak mn'eh ih iz-b'eh-ZHAT'?

Are there any potholes I need to avoid?
Есть ли какие-нибудь выбоины, которых мне следует избегать?
Jehst' l'i ka-K'I-jeh-n'i-but' VY-bə-i-ny, ka-TO-ryh mn'eh SL'EH-du-jeht iz-b'eh-GAT'?

How fast are you going?
С какой скоростью вы едете?
S ka-KOJ SKO-rəs-t'u vy JEH-d'eh-t'eh?

Do I need to put my emergency blinkers on?

Я должен/должна включить аварийные огни?

Ja DOL-zhehn/dal-ZHNA fkl'u-CHIT' ava-RIJ-ny-jeh ag-N'I?

Make sure to use the right turn signals.

Не забудьте включить правый «поворотник».

N'eh za-BUT'-t'eh fkl'u-CHIT' PRA-vyj pa-va-ROT-n'ik.

We need a good mechanic.

Нам нужен хороший механик.

Nam NU-zhehn ha-RO-shyj m'eh-HA-n'ic.

Can we get a push?

Не могли бы вы помочь нам подтолкнуть машину?

N'eh mag-L'I by vy pa-MOCH' nam pat-tal-KNUT' ma-SHY-nu?

I have to call the towing company to move my car.

Мне нужно вызвать эвакуатор, чтобы отвезти свою машину.

Mn'eh NUZH-nə VYZ-vat' eh-va-ku-A-tər, SHTO-by at-v'ehs-T'I sva-ju ma-SHY-nu.

Make sure to check the battery and spark plugs for any problems.

Не забудьте проверить аккумулятор и свечи зажигания на наличие проблем.

N'eh za-BUT'-t'eh pra-V'EH-r'it' aku-mu-L'A-tər i SV'EH-chi za-zhy-GA-n'i-ja na na-L'I-chi-jeh prab-L'EHM.

Check the oil level.

Проверьте уровень масла.

Pra-V'EHR'-t'eh U-rə-vən' MAS-lə.

I need to notify my insurance company.

Я должен/должна сообщить в свою страховую компанию.

Ja DOL-zhehn/dal-ZNNA sa-ab-SCHIT' f sva-JU stra-ha-VU-ju kam-PA-n'i-ju.

When do I pay the taxi driver?

Когда я должен/должна заплатить таксисту?

Kag-DA ja DOL'zhehn/dal-ZHNA zap-la-T'IT' tak-S'IS-tu?

Please take me to the nearest train station.

Пожалуйста, отвезите меня на ближайший железнодорожный вокзал.

Pa-ZHA-ləs-tə, at-v'eh-Z'I-t'eh m'eh-N'A na bl'i-ZHAJ-shyj zheh-l'eh-zna-da-ROZH-nyj vak-ZAL.

How long does it take to get to this address?
Сколько времени нужно, чтобы добраться до этого адреса?
SKOL'-kə VR'EH-m'eh-n'i NUZH-nə, SHTO-by dab-RA-tsa də EH-tə-və AD-r'eh-sa?

Can you stop here, please?
Остановитесь здесь, пожалуйста.
As-ta-na-V'I-t'ehs' zd'ehs', pa-ZHA-ləs-tə.

You can drop me off anywhere around here.
Вы можете высадить меня где-нибудь здесь.
Vy MO-zheh-t'eh VY-sa-d'it' m'eh-N'A GD'EH-n'i-but' zd'ehs'.

Is there a charge for extra passengers?
Нужно платить за дополнительных пассажиров?
NU-zhnə pla-T'IT' za da-pal-N'I-t'ehl'-nyh pa-sa-ZHY-rəf?

What is the condition of the road? Is it safe to travel there?
В каком состоянии дорога? По ней безопасно ездить?
F ka-KOM sas-ta-JA-n'i-i da-RO-ga? Pa n'ehj b'eh-za-PAS-nə JEHZ-d'it'?

Take me to the emergency room.
Отвезите меня в отделение скорой помощи.
At-v'eh-Z'I-t'eh m'eh-N'A v at-d'eh-L'EH-n'i-jeh SKO-rəj PO-ma-schi.

Take me to the embassy.
Отвезите меня в посольство.
At-v'eh-Z'I-t'eh m'eh-N'A f pa-SOL'-stvə.

I want to travel around the country.
Я хочу попутешествовать по стране.
Ja ha-CHU pa-pu-t'eh-SHEH-stvə-vət' pa stra-N'EH.

Is this the right side of the road?
Это правая сторона дороги?
EH-tə PRA-va-ja sta-ra-NA da-RO-g'i?

My car broke down, please help!
Моя машина сломалась, пожалуйста, помогите!
Ma-JA ma-SHY-na sla-MA-las', pa-ZHA-ləs-tə, pa-ma-G'I-t'eh!

Can you help me change my tire?
Не могли бы вы помочь мне заменить колесо?
N'eh mag-L'I by vy pa-MOCH mn'eh za-m'eh-n'iT' ka-l'eh-SO?

Where can I get a rental car?

Где я могу арендовать машину?

Gd'eh ja ma-GU ar'ehn-da-VAT' ma-SHY-nu?

Please take us to the hospital.

Пожалуйста, отвезите нас в больницу.

Pa-ZHA-ləs-tə, at-v'eh-Z'I-t'eh nas v bal'-N'I-tsu.

Is that the car rental office?

Это прокат автомобилей?

EH-tə pra-KAT af-ta-ma-B'I-l'ehj?

May I have a price list for your fleet?

Могу я посмотреть цены на ваши автомобили?

Ma-GU ja pas-mat-R'EHT' TSEH-ny na VA-shy af-ta-ma-B'I-l'i?

Can I get insurance on this rental car?

Могу я взять страховку на этот прокатный автомобиль?

Ma-GU ja vz'at' stra-HOF-ku na EH-tət pra-KAT-nyj af-ta-ma-B'IL'?

How much is the car per day?

Сколько стоит автомобиль в день?

SKOL'-kə STO-it af-ta-ma-B'IL' v d'ehn'?

How many kilometers can I travel with this car?

Сколько километров я могу проехать на этой машине?

SKOL'-kə k'i-la'-M'EH-trəf ja ma-GU pra-JEH-hat' na EH-taj ma-SHY-n'eh?

I would like maps of the region if you have them.

Я хотел/хотела бы получить карты этой местности, если они у вас есть.

Ja ha-T'EHL/ha-T'EH-la by pa-lu-CH'IT' KAR-ty EH-təj M'EHS-nəs-t'i, JEHS-l'i a-n'i u vas jehst'.

When I am done with the car, where do I return it?

Куда мне сдать машину, когда я окончу поездку?

Ku-DA mn'eh zdat' ma-SHY-nu, kag-DA ja za-KON-chu pa-JEH-stku?

Is this a standard or automatic transmission?

Это ручная или автоматическая коробка передач?

EH-tə ruch-NA-ja I-l'i af-ta-ma-T'I-ch'ehs-ka-ja ka-ROP-ka p'eh-r'eh-DACH?

Is this car gas-efficient? How many kilometers per liter?
Это экономичный автомобиль? Сколько литров на километр?
Eh-tə eh-ka-na-M'ICH-nyj af-ta-ma-B'IL'? SKOL'-kə L'IT-rəf na k'i-la-M'EHTR?

Where is the spare tire stored?
Где хранится запасное колесо?
Gd'eh hra-N'I-tsa za-pas-NO-jeh ka-l'eh-SO?

Are there places around the city that are difficult to drive?
Есть ли в городе места, где трудно ездить?
Jehst' li v GO-rə-de m'ehs-TA, gd'eh TRU-dnə JEHZ-d'it'?

At what time of the day is the traffic the worst?
В какое время движение наиболее загруженное?
F ka-KO-jeh VR'EH-m'a dv'i-ZHEH-n'i-jeh na-i-BO-l'eh-jeh zag-RU-zheh-na-jeh?

We can't park right here.
Мы не можем припарковаться здесь.
My n'eh MO-zhehm pr'i-par-ka-VA-tsa PR'A-mə zd'ehs'.

What is the speed limit?
Какое здесь ограничение скорости?
Ka-KO-jeh zd'ehs' ag-ra-n'i-CHEH-n'i-jeh SKO-rəs-t'i?

Keep the change.
Оставьте сдачу себе.
Os-TAF'-t'eh ZDA-chu s'eh-B'EH.

Now let's get off here.
Давайте сойдём здесь.
Da-VAJ-t'eh saj-D'OM zd'ehs'.

Where is the train station?
Где находится железнодорожный вокзал?
Gd'eh na-HO-d'i-tsa zheh-L'EHZ-nə-da-ROZH-nyj vak-ZAL?

Is the bus stop nearby?
Автобусная остановка рядом?
Af-TO-bus-na-ja as-ta-NOF-kə R'A-dəm?

When does the bus run?
Когда ходит автобус?
Kag-DA HO-d'it af-TO-bus?

Where do I go to catch a taxi?

Где я могу поймать такси?

Gd'eh ja ma-GU paj-MAT' tak-S'I?

Does the train go to the north station?

Поезд идет на Северный вокзал?

PO-jehst i-D'OT na S'EH-v'ehr-nyj vak-ZAL?

Where do I go to purchase tickets?

Где я могу купить билеты?

Gd'eh ja ma-GU ku-P'IT' b'i-L'EH-ty?

How much is a ticket to Moscow?

Сколько стоит билет до Москвы?

SKOL'-kə STO-it b'i-L'EHT da mas-KVY?

What is the next stop along this route?

Какая следующая остановка на этом маршруте?

Ka-KA-ja SL'EH-du-scha-ja as-ta-NOF-ka na EH-təm mar-SHRU-t'eh?

Can I have a ticket to Moscow?

Можно мне билет до Москвы?

MOZH-nə mn'eh b'i-L'EHT da Mas-KVY?

Where is my designated platform?

Где находится моя посадочная платформа?

Gd'eh na-HO-d'i-tsa ma-JA pa-SA-dach-na-JA plat-FOR-ma?

Where do I place my luggage?

Куда я могу положить свой багаж?

Ku-DA ja ma-GU pa-la-ZHYT' svoj ba-GAZH?

Are there any planned closures today?

Сегодня планируется закрытие дорог?

S'eh-VO-dn'a pla-N'I-ru-jeh-tsa zak-RY-t'i-jeh da-ROG?

Where are the machines that disperse tickets?

Где находятся автоматы с билетами?

Gd'eh na-HO-d'a-tsa af-ta-MA-ty z b'i-L'HE-ta-m'i?

Does this car come with insurance?

Эта машина со страховкой?

EH-tə ma-SHY-na sa stra-HOF-kəj?

May I have a timetable, please?
Можно мне расписание, пожалуйста?
MOZH-nə mn'eh ras-p'i-SA-n'i-jeh, pa-ZHA-ləs-tə?

How often do trains come to this area?
Как часто сюда ходят поезда?
Kak CHAS-tə s'u-DA HO-d'at pa-jeh-ZDA?

Is the train running late?
Поезд опаздывает?
PO-jehst a-PAZ-dy-va-jeht?

Has the train been cancelled?
Поезд отменили?
PO-jehst at-m'eh-N'I-l'i?

Is this seat available?
Это место свободно?
Eh-tə M'EHS-tə sva-BOD-nə?

Do you mind if I sit here?
Вы не возражаете, если я сяду сюда?
Vy n'eh vaz-ra-ZHA-j'eh-t'eh, JEHS-l'i ja S'A-du s'u-DA?

I've lost my ticket.
Я потерял/потеряла билет.
Ja pa-t'eh-R'AL/pa-t'eh-R'A-la bi-L'EHT.

Excuse me, this is my stop.
Извините, это моя остановка.
Iz-v'i-N'I-t'eh, EH-tə ma-JA as-ta-NOF-ka.

Can you please open the window?
Не могли бы вы открыть окно?
N'eh mag-L'I by vy at-KRYT' ak-NO?

Is smoking allowed in the car?
В вагоне разрешено курить?
V va-GO-n'eh raz-r'eh-sheh-NO ku-R'IT'?

Wait, my luggage is still on board!
Подождите, мой багаж ещё не выгрузили!
Pa-dazh-D'I-t'eh, moj ba-GASH jeh-SCH'O n'eh VYG-ru-z'i-l'i!

70

Where can I get a map?

Где я могу взять карту?

Gd'eh ja ma-GU vz'at' KAR-tu?

What zone is this?

Какая это зона?

Ka-KA-ja EH-tə ZO-na?

Please keep your distance!

Пожалуйста, держите дистанцию!

Pa-ZHA-ləs-tə, d'ehr-ZHY-t'eh d'is-TAN-tsy-ju!

I am about to run out of gas.

У меня скоро кончится топливо.

U m'eh-N'A SKO-rə KON-ch'it-tsa TOP-l'i-və.

My tank is halfway full.

Мой бак заполнен наполовину.

Moj bak za-POL-n'ehn na-pa-la-V'I-nu.

What type of gas does this car take?

На каком топливе ездит эта машина?

Na ka-KOM TOP-l'i-v'eh JEHZ-d'it EH-tə ma-SHY-na?

There is gas leaking out of my car.

У меня из машины течёт топливо.

U m'eh-N'A iz ma-SHY-ny t'eh-CH'OT TOP-l'i-və.

Fill up the tank.

Заправьте машину.

Zap-RAF'-t'eh ma-SHY-nu.

There is no more gas in my car.

У меня закончилось топливо.

U m'eh-N'A za-KON-ch'i-ləs' TOP-l'i-və.

Where can I find the nearest gas station?

Где находится ближайшая заправка?

Gd'eh na-HO-d'i-tsa bl'i-ZHAJ-sha-ja zap-RAF-ka?

The engine light for my car is on.

У меня загорелась лампочка «проверьте двигатель».

U m'eh-N'A za-ga-R'EH-las' LAM-pach-ka "pra-V'EHR'-t'eh DV'I-ga-t'ehl".

Do you mind if I drive?

Вы не возражаете, если я поведу машину?

Vy n'eh vaz-ra-ZHA-j'eh-t'eh, JEHS-l'i ja pa-v'eh-DU ma-SHY-nu?

Please get in the back seat.

Пожалуйста, садитесь сзади.

Pa-ZHA-ləs-tə, sa-D'I-t'ehs' ZZA-d'i.

Let me get my bags out before you leave.

Позвольте мне забрать свой багаж, прежде чем вы уедете.

Paz-VOL'-t'eh mn'eh zab-RAT' svoj ba-GASH, PR'EH-zhd'eh ch'ehm vy u-JEH-d'eh-t'eh.

The weather is bad, please drive slowly.

Погода плохая, пожалуйста, едьте тихо.

Pa-GO-da pla-HA-ja, pa-ZHA-ləs-tə, JEHT'-t'eh T'I-hə.

Our vehicle isn't equipped to travel there.

Наша машина не сможет там проехать.

NA-sha ma-SHY-na n'eh SMO-zheht tam pra-JEH-hat'.

One ticket to the north, please.

Один билет на север, пожалуйста.

A-D'IN b'i-L'EHT na S'EH-v'ehr, pa-ZHA-ləs-tə.

If you get lost, call me.

Если заблудитесь, позвоните мне.

JEH-sl'i zab-LU-d'i-t'ehs', paz-va-N'I-t'eh mn'eh.

That bus is overcrowded. I'll wait for the next one.

Автобус переполнен. Я подожду следующего.

Af-TO-bus p'eh-r'eh-POL-n'ehn. Ja pa-dazh-DU SL'EH-du-sch'eh-və.

Please, take my seat.

Пожалуйста, садитесь на моё место.

Pa-ZHA-ləs-tə, sa-D'I-t'ehs' na ma-JO M'EHS-tə.

Ma'am, I think your stop is coming up.

Девушка, я думаю, скоро ваша остановка.

D'EH-vush-ka, ja DU-ma-ju, SKO-rə VA-sha as-ta-NOF-ka.

Wake me up when we get to our destination.

Разбудите меня, когда мы прибудем.

Raz-bu-D'I-t'eh m'eh-N'A, kag-DA my pr'i-BU-d'ehm.

I would like to purchase a travel pass for the entire day.

Я бы хотел/хотела купить проездной на весь день.

Ja by ha-T'EHL/ha-T'EH-la ku-P'IT' pra-jehz-NOJ na v'ehs' d'ehn'.

Would you like to swap seats with me?

Хотите поменяться со мной местами?

Ha-T'I-t'eh pa-m'eh-N'A-tsa sa mnoj m'ehs-TA-m'i?

I want to sit with my family.

Я хочу сидеть со своей семьей.

Ja ha-CHU s'i-D'HET' sa sva-JEHJ s'ehm-JOJ.

I would like a window seat for this trip.

На время поездки я бы хотел/хотела место у окна.

Na VR'EH-m'a pa-JEHS-Tk'i ja by ha-T'EHL/ha-T'EH-la M'EHS-tə u ak-NA.

RELIGIOUS QUESTIONS

Where can I go to pray?

Куда я могу пойти, чтобы помолиться?

Ku-DA ja ma-GU paj-T'I, SHTO-by pa-ma-L'I-tsa?

What services does your church offer?

Какие услуги предлагает ваша церковь?

Ka-K'I-jeh us-LU-g'i pr'eh-dla-GA-JEHT VA-sha TSEHR-kəf'?

Are you non-denominational?

Вы межконфессиональны?

Vy m'ehsh-kan-f'eh-s'i-a-NAL'-ny?

Is there a shuttle to your church?

До вашей церкви есть подвоз?

Da VA-shej TSEH-rkv'i jehst' pad-VOZ?

How long does church last?

Сколько длится служба?

SKOL'-ka DL'I-tsa SLUZH-ba?

Where is your bathroom?

Где у вас уборная?

Gd'eh u vas u-BOR-na-ya?

What should I wear to your services?

Во что я должен/должна быть одет/одета у вас на службе?

Va shto ja DOL-zhehn/dal-ZHNA byt' a-D'EHT/a-D'EH-ta u vas na SLUZH-b'eh?

Where is the nearest Catholic church?

Где находится ближайшая католическая церковь?

Gd'eh na-HO-d'i-tsa bl'i-ZHAJ-sha-ja ka-ta-L'I-ch'ehs-ka-ja TSEHR-kəf'?

Where is the nearest mosque?

Где находится ближайшая мечеть?

Gd'eh na-HO-d'i-tsa bl'i-ZHAJ-sha-ja m'eh-CHEHT'?

Does your church perform weddings?
Ваша церковь проводит свадебные торжества?

VA-sha TS'EHR-kəf' pra-VO-d'it SVA-d'ehb-ny-jeh tar-zheh-STVA?

Who is getting married?
Кто женится?

Kto ZHEH-n'i-tsa?

Will our marriage license be legal if we leave the country?
Наше свидетельство о браке будет законным, если мы уедем из страны?

NA-sheh sv'i-D'EH-t'ehl'-stvə ə BRA-k'eh BU-d'eht za-KON-nym, JEH-sl'I my u-JEH-d'ehm is stra-NY?

Where do we get our marriage license?
Где мы можем забрать наше свидетельство о браке?

Gd'eh my MO-zhem zab-RAT' NA-sheh sv'i-D'EH-t'ehl'-stvə ə BRA-k'eh?

What is the charge for marrying us?
Сколько стоит венчание?

SKOL'-kə STO-it v'ehn-CHA-n'i-jeh?

Do you handle same-sex marriage?
Вы заключаете однополые браки?

Vy zak-l'u-CHA-j'eh-t'eh ad-na-PO-ly-jeh BRA-k'i?

Please gather here to pray.
Пожалуйста, соберитесь здесь для молитвы.

Pa-ZHA-ləs-tə, sa-b'eh-R'I-t'ehs' zd'ehs' dl'a ma-L'IT-vy.

I would like to lead a sermon.
Я бы хотел/хотела прочесть проповедь.

Ja by ha-T'EHL/ha-T'EH-la pra-CH'EHST' PRO-pə-v'eht'.

I would like to help with prayer.
Я бы хотел/хотела помочь с молитвой.

Ja by ha-T'EHL/ha-T'EH-la pa-MOCH s ma-l'IT-vəj.

How should I dress before arriving?
Как мне одеться?

Kak mn'eh a-D'EH-tsa?

What are your rules?
Какие у вас правила?

Ka-K'I-jeh u vas PRA-v'i-la?

Are cell phones allowed in your building?

В вашем здании разрешены мобильные телефоны?

V VA-sh'ehm ZDA-n'i-i raz-r'eh-sheh-NY ma-B'IL'-ny-jeh t'eh-l'eh-FO-ny?

I plan on bringing my family this Sunday.

Я планирую взять с собой семью в это воскресенье.

Ja pla-N'I-ru-ju vz'at' s sa-BOJ s'ehm-JU v EH-tə vas-kr'eh-S'EHN'-jeh.

Do you accept donations?

Вы принимаете пожертвования?

Vy pr'i-n'i-MA-j'eh-t'eh pa-ZHEHR-tvə-və-n'i-ja?

I would like to offer my time to your cause.

Я бы хотел/хотела предложить свою помощь в вашем вопросе.

Ya by ha-T'EHL/ha-T'EH-la pr'eh-dla-ZHYT' sva-YU PO-məsch v VA-shehm vap-RO-s'eh.

What book should I be reading from?

Из какой книги мне читать?

Is ka-KOJ KN'I-g'i mn'eh ch'i-TAT'?

Do you have a gift store?

У вас есть сувенирная лавка?

U vas jehst' su-v'eh-N'IR-na-ja LAF-ka?

EMERGENCY

I need help over here!
Сюда, мне нужна помощь!
S'u-DA, mn'eh nuzh-NA PO-mastch!

I'm lost, please help me.
Я заблудился/заблудилась, пожалуйста, помогите мне.
Ja zab-lu-D'IL-s'a/za-blu-D'I-las', pa-ZHA-ləs-tə, pa-ma-G'I-t'eh mn'eh.

Someone call the police!
Вызовите полицию!
VY-zə-v'i-t'eh pa-L'I-tsy-ju!

Is there a lawyer who speaks English?
Здесь есть адвокат, который говорит по-английски?
Zd'ehs' jehst' ad-və-KAT, ka-TO-ryj ga-va-R'IT pa-an-GL'I-sk'i?

Please help, my car doesn't work.
Пожалуйста, помогите мне, моя машина сломалась.
Pa-ZHA-ləs-tə, pa-ma-G'I-t'eh mn'eh, ma-JA ma-SHY-na sla-MA-las'.

There was a collision!
Произошла авария!
Pra-i-za-sh-LA a-VA-r'i-ja!

Call an ambulance!
Вызовите скорую!
VY-zə-v'i-t'eh SKO-ru-ju!

Am I under arrest?
Я арестован/арестована?
Ja ar'ehs-TO-vən/ar'ehs-TO-və-nə?

I need an interpreter, this is an emergency!
Мне нужен переводчик, это срочно!
Mn'eh NU-zhen p'eh-r'eh-VOT-chik, EH-tə SROCH-nə!

My back hurts.
У меня болит спина.
U m'eh-N'A ba-L'IT sp'i-NA.

Is there an American consulate here?
Здесь есть американское консульство?
Zd'ehs' jehst' a-m'eh-r'i-KAN-skə-jeh KON-sul'-stvə?

I'm sick and don't feel too well.
Меня тошнит, и я плохо себя чувствую.
M'eh-N'A tash-N'IT, i ja PLO-hə se-B'A CHUS-tvu-ju.

Is there a pharmacy where I can get medicine?
Здесь есть аптека, где я могу купить лекарства?
Zd'ehs 'jehst' ap-T'EH-ka, gd'eh ja ma-GU ku-P'IT' l'eh-KAR-stvə?

I need a doctor immediately.
Мне срочно нужен врач.
Mn'eh SROCH-nə NU-zhehn vrach.

I have a tooth missing.
У меня выпал зуб.
U m'eh-N'A VY-pəl zup.

Please! Someone bring my child to me!
Пожалуйста! Кто-нибудь верните мне моего ребёнка!
Pa-ZHA-ləs-tə! KTO-n'i-but' v'ehr-n'i-t'eh mn'eh ma-jeh-VO r'eh-B'O-nkə!

Where does it hurt?
Где у вас болит?
Gd'eh u vas ba-L'IT?

Hold on to me!
Держитесь за меня!
D'ehr-ZHY-t'ehs' za m'eh-N'A!

There's an emergency!
Чрезвычайная ситуация!
CHR'EH-zvy-chaj-na-ja s'i-tu-A-tsy-ja!

I need a telephone to call for help.
Мне нужен телефон, чтобы вызвать помощь.
Mn'eh NU-zhehn t'eh-l'eh-FON, SHTO-by VYZ-vət' PO-məsch.

My nose is bleeding.

У меня из носа течёт кровь.

U m'eh-N'A iz NO-sa t'eh-CH'OT krof'.

I twisted my ankle.

Я подвернул/подвернула ногу.

Ja pad-v'ehr-NUL/pad-v'ehr-NU'lə NO-gu.

I don't feel so good.

Я плохо себя чувствую.

Ja PLO-hə s'eh-B'A CHUS-tvu-ju.

Don't move, please.

Не двигайтесь, пожалуйста.

N'eh DV'I-gaj-t'ehs', pa-ZHA-ləs-tə.

Hello operator, can I place a collect call?

Алло, оператор, могу я сделать звонок за счёт вызываемого абонента?

A-LO, a-p'he-RA-tər, ma-GU ja ZD'EH-lat' zva-NOK za sch'ot vy-zy-VA-jeh-mə-və a-ba-N'EHN-ta?

I'll get a doctor for you.

Я вызову вам врача.

Ja VY-zə-vu vam vra-CHA.

Please hold my passports for a while.

Пожалуйста, подержите немного мои документы.

Pa-ZHA-ləs-tə, pa-d'ehr-ZHY-t'eh n'hem-NO-gə ma-I da-ku-M'EHN-ty.

I lost my wallet.

Я потерял/потеряла кошелёк.

Ja pa-t'ehr-YAL/pa-t'eh-R'A-la ka-sheh-L'OK.

I have a condition! Please check my wallet.

У меня есть заболевание! Пожалуйста, посмотрите у меня в бумажнике.

U m'eh-N'A jehst' za-ba-l'he-VA-n'i-jeh! Pa-ZHA-ləs-tə, pas-mat-R'I-t'eh u m'eh-N'A v bu-MAZH-n'i-k'eh.

My wife is in labor, please help!

Моя жена рожает, пожалуйста, помогите!

Ma-JA zheh-NA ra-ZHA-jeht, pa-ZHA-ləs-tə, pa-ma-G'I-t'eh!

I would like to talk to my lawyer.
Я бы хотел/хотела поговорить с моим адвокатом.
Ja by ha-T'EHL/ha-T'EH-la pa-ga-va-R'IT' s ma-IM ad-va-KA-təm.

It's an earthquake!
Это землетрясение!
EH-tə z'ehm-l'eh-tr'a-S'EH-n'i-jeh!

Get under the desk and protect your head.
Спрячьтесь под стол и закройте голову.
SPR'A-cht'ehs' pat stol i zak-ROJ-t'eh GO-lə-vu.

How can I help you?
Чем я могу вам помочь?
Ch'ehm ja ma-GU vam pa-MOCH?

Everyone, he needs help!
Люди, ему нужна помощь!
L'U-d'i, jeh-MU nuzh-NA PO-məsch!

Yes, help me get an ambulance.
Да, помогите мне вызвать скорую.
Da, pa-ma-G'I-t'eh mn'eh VYZ-vət' SKO-ru-ju.

Thank you, but I am fine. Please don't help me.
Спасибо, но я в порядке. Пожалуйста, не нужно мне помогать.
Spa-S'I-bə, no ja f pa-R'AT-k'e. N'eh NUZH-nə mn'eh pa-ma-GAT'.

I need help carrying this injured person.
Мне нужна помощь, чтобы перенести этого раненого.
Mn'eh nuzh-NA PO-məsch, SHTO-by p'eh-r'eh-nes-T'I EH-tə-və RA-n'eh-nə-və.

TECHNOLOGY

What is the country's official website?
Какой официальный сайт страны?
Ka-KOJ a-f'i-tsy-AL'-nyj sajt stra-NY?

Do you know the name of a good wi-fi café?
Вы знаете хорошее wi-fi кафе?
Vy ZNA-j'eh-t'eh ha-RO-sheh-jeh vaj-FAJ ka-FEH?

Do you have any experience with computers?
У вас есть опыт работы с компьютерами?
U vas jehst' O-pyt ra-BO-ty s kam-PJU-t'eh-rə-m'i?

How well do you know Apple products?
Как хорошо вы знакомы с продуктами Apple?
Kak ha-ra-SHO vy zna-KO-my s pra-DUK-tə-m'i ehpl?

What kind of work did you do with computers?
Какую работу вы делали на компьютере?
Ka-KU-ju ra-BO-tu vy D'EH-la-l'i na kam-PJU-tə-r'eh?

Are you a programmer?
Вы программист?
Vy prag-ra-M'IST?

Are you a developer?
Вы разработчик?
Vy raz-ra-BOT-chik?

I want to use this computer instead of that one.
Я хочу использовать вот этот компьютер вместо этого.
Ja ha-CHU is-POL'-zə-vət' vot EH-tət kam-PJU-tər VM'EHS-tə EH-tə-va.

Do you know where I can buy discount computer parts?
Вы знаете, где я могу купить детали для компьютера со скидкой?
Vy ZNA-j'eh-t'eh gd'eh ja ma-GU ku-P'IT' d'e-TA-l'i dl'a kam-PJU-tə-rə sa SK'IT-kəj?

I have ten years of experience with Windows.
У меня десятилетний опыт работы с Windows.
U m'eh-N'A d'he-s'a-t'i-L'EHT-n'ij O-pyt ra-BO-ty s V'IN-do-us.

What is the wi-fi password?
Какой пароль от wi-fi?
Ka-KOJ pa-ROL' at vaj-FA-ja?

I need to have my login information reset.
Мне нужно сбросить данные для входа.
Mn'eh NUZH-nə SBRO-s'it' DAN-ny-jeh dl'a FHO-da.

The hard drive is making a clicking noise.
Жёсткий диск издаёт звук щелчка.
ZHOS-kij d'isk iz-da-JOT zvuk sch'ehl-CHKA.

How do I uninstall this program from my device?
Как мне удалить эту программу с моего устройства?
Kak mn'eh u-da-L'IT' EH-tu prag-RA-mu s ma-jeh-VO us-TROJ-stvə?

Can you help me set up a new account with this website?
Вы можете помочь мне зарегистрироваться на этом сайте?
Vy MO-zheh-t'eh pa-MOCH mn'eh za-r'eh-g'is-TR'I-rə-va-tsa na EH-təm SAJ-t'eh?

Why is the internet so slow?
Почему интернет такой медленный?
Pa-ch'eh-MU in-t'ehr-NEHT ta-KOJ M'EHD-l'eh-nyj?

Why is YouTube buffering every video I play?
Почему YouTube запоминает все видео, которые я просматриваю?
Pa-ch'eh-MU ju-TUB za-pa-m'i-NA-jeht fs'eh V'I-d'eh-o, ka-TO-ry-jeh ja pras-MAT-tr'i-va-ju?

My web camera isn't displaying a picture.
Моя веб-камера не отображает изображения.
Ma-JA vehb-KA-m'eh-ra n'eh a-tab-ra-ZHA-jeht i-zab-ra-ZHEH-n'i-ja.

I have no bars on my phone.
У меня разряжен телефон.
U m'eh-N'A raz-RYA-zhen t'eh-l'eh-FON.

Where can I get my phone serviced?
Где я могу починить телефон?
Gd'eh ja ma-GU pa-chi-N'IT' t'eh-l'eh-FON?

My phone shows that it is charging but won't charge.

Мой телефон показывает, что зарядка идёт, но он не заряжается.

Moj t'eh-l'eh-FON pa-KA-zy-va-jeht, shto za-R'AT-kə i-D'OT, no on n'eh za-r'a-ZHA-jeh-tsa.

I think someone else is controlling my computer.

Мне кажется, кто-то управляет моим компьютером.

Mn'eh KA-zheh-tsa, KTO-tə up-rav-L'A-jeht ma-IM kam-PJU-tə-rəm.

My computer just gave a blue screen and shut down.

На моём компьютере только что появился голубой экран, и он выключился.

Na ma-JOM kam-PJU-tə-re TOL'-kə shto pa-ja-V'IL-s'a ga-lu-BOJ ehk-RAN, i on VY-kl'u-chil-s'a.

Do you have the battery for this laptop?

У вас есть аккумулятор для этого ноутбука?

U vas jehst' a-ku-mu-L'A-tər dl'a EH-tə-və nout-BU-ka?

Where can I get a compatible adapter?

Где я могу купить подходящий адаптер?

Gd'eh ja ma-GU ku-P'IT' pat-ha-D'A-schij a-DAP-t'ehr?

I can't get online with the information you gave me.

Я не могу подключиться к интернету с информацией, которую вы мне дали.

Ja n'eh ma-GU pat-kl'u-CHI-tsa k in-t'ehr-NEH-tu s in-far-MA-tsy-jehj, ka-TO-ru-ju vy mn'eh DA-l'i.

This keyboard is not working correctly.

Эта клавиатура работает неправильно.

Eh-tə kla-v'i-a-TU-ra ra-BO-ta-jeht n'eh PRA-v'il'-nə.

What is the login information for this computer?

Какой логин и пароль для этого компьютера?

Ka-KOJ LO-g'in i pa-ROL' dl'a EH-tə-və kam-PJU-tə-rə?

I need you to update my computer.

Мне нужно, чтобы вы обновили мой компьютер.

Mn'eh NUZH-nə, SHTO-by vy ab-na-V'I-l'i moj kam-PJU-tər.

Can you build my website?

Вы можете создать мне веб-сайт?

Vy MO-zheh-t'eh saz-DAT' mn'eh vehp-SAJT?

I prefer Wordpress.

Я предпочитаю Wordpress.

Ja pr'eht-pa-chi-TA-ju vord-PR'EHS.

What are your rates per hour?

Какова ваша почасовая ставка?

Ka-ka-VA VA-sha pa-cha-sa-VA-ja STAF-ka?

Do you have experience handling email servers?

У вас есть опыт управления почтовыми серверами?

U vas jehst' O-pyt up-rav-L'EH-n'i-ja pach-TO-vy-m'i s'ehr-v'eh-RA-m'i?

I am locked out of my account, can you help?

Мой аккаунт заблокирован, вы можете мне помочь?

Moj a-KA-unt zab-la-K'I-rə-vən, vy MO-zheh-t'eh mn'eh pa-MOCH?

None of the emails I am sending are going through.

Ни одно из писем, которые я отправляю, не доходят до адресата.

N'i ad-NO is P'I-s'ehm, ka-TO-ry-jeh ja at-prav-L'A-ju, n'eh da-HO-d'at da ad-r'eh-SA-ta.

The time and date on my computer are wrong.

Время и дата на моём компьютере неправильные.

VR'EH-m'a i DA-ta na ma-JOM kam-PJU-tə-r'ə n'eh-PRA-v'il'-ny-jeh.

Is this game free to play?

Эта игра бесплатная?

EH-tə ig-RA b'ehs-PLAT-na-ja?

Where do I go to download the client?

Где я могу скачать клиент?

Gd'eh ja ma-GU ska-CHAT' kl'i-JEHNT?

I am having troubles chatting with my family.

У меня проблемы при общении с семьёй.

U m'eh-N'A prab-L'EH-my pr'i ap-SCH'EH-n'i-I s s'ehm-JOJ.

Is this the fastest computer here?

Это самый быстрый компьютер здесь?

EH-tə SA-myj BYS-tryj kam-PJU-tər zd'ehs'?

How much space is on the computer?

Сколько места на этом компьютере?

SKOL'-kə M'EHS-tə na EH-təm kam-PJU-tə-r'e?

Will my profile be deleted once I log out? Or does it save?

Мой профиль будет удалён, когда я выйду из системы? Или он сохранится?

Moj PRO-f'il' BU-d'het u-da-L'ON kag-DA ja VYJ-du is s'is-T'EH-my? I-l'i on sah-ra-N'I-tsa?

How much do you charge for computer use?

Сколько стоит использование компьютера?

SKOL'-kə STO-it is-POL'-zə-və-n'i-jeh kam-PJU-tə-ra?

Are group discounts offered?

Вы предлагаете групповые скидки?

Vy pred-la-GA-j'eh-t'eh gru-pa-VY-jeh SKIT-k'i?

Can I use my own headphones with your computer?

Могу я использовать свои наушники с вашим компьютером?

Ma-GU ja is-POL'-zə-vat' sva-I na-USH-n'ik'i s VA-shym kam-PJU-tə-rəm?

Do you have a data cap?

У вас есть ограничение по данным?

U vas jehst' ag-ra-n'i-CHEH-n'i-jeh pa DAN-nym?

I think this computer has a virus.

Я думаю, на этом компьютере есть вирус.

Ja DU-ma-ju, na EH-təm kam-PJU-tə-r'eh jehst' V'I-rus.

The battery for my laptop is running low.

У моего ноутбука садится батарея.

U ma-jeh-VO nout-BU-ka sa-D'I-tsa ba-ta-R'EH-ja.

Where can I plug this in? I need to recharge my device.

Где я могу подключиться к сети? Мне нужно зарядить своё устройство.

Gd'eh ja ma-GU pat-kl'u-CHI-tsa k s'eh-T'I? Mn'eh NUZH-nə za-r'a-D'IT' sva-JO us-TROJ-stvə.

Do you have a mini-USB cord?

У вас есть mini-USB кабель?

U vas jehst' M'I-n'i ju-ehs-B'I KA-b'ehl'?

Where can I go to watch the game?

Куда я могу пойти, чтобы посмотреть игру?

Ku-DA ja ma-GU paj-T'I, SHTO-by pas-mat-R'EHT' ig-RU?

Do you have an iPhone charger?

У вас есть зарядное устройство для iPhone?

U vas jehst' za-R'A-dna-jeh us-TROJ-stvə dl'a aj-FO-na?

I need a new battery for my watch.

Мне нужна новая батарейка для часов.

Mn'eh nuzh-NA NO-va-ja ba-ta-R'EHJ-ka dl'a ma-IH cha-SOF.

I need to borrow an HDMI cord.

Мне нужно одолжить HDMI шнур.

Mn'eh NUZH-nə a-dal-ZHYT' HDMI shnur.

What happens when I exceed the data cap?

Что случится, если я превышу ограничение по данным?

Shto slu-CHI-tsa, JEH-sl'I ja pr'eh-VY-shu ag-ra-n'i-CH'EH-n'i-jeh pa DAN-nym?

Can you help me pair my Bluetooth device?

Вы можете помочь мне подключить моё Bluetooth устройство?

Vy MO-zheh-t'eh pa-MOCH mn'eh pat-kl'u-CHIT' ma-JO Bluetooth us-TROJ-stvə?

I need a longer ethernet cord.

Мне нужен более длинный кабель Ethernet.

Mn'eh NU-zhehn BO-l'eh-jeh DL'IN-nyj KA-b'ehl' Ethernet.

Why is this website restricted?

Почему доступ к этому сайту ограничен?

Pa-ch'eh-MU DOS-tup k EH-tə-mu SAJ-tu ag-ra-N'I-ch'ehn?

How can I unblock this website?

Как я могу разблокировать этот сайт?

Kak ja ma-GU raz-bla-K'I-rə-vət' EH-tət sajt?

Is that television 4k or higher?

Разрешение этого телевизора 4 тысячи или больше?

Raz-r'eh-SHEH-n'i-jeh EH-tə-və t'eh-l'eh-V'I-'zə-rə ch'eh-TY-r'eh TY-s'a-chi I-l'I BOL'sheh?

Do you have the Office suite on this computer?

У вас есть пакет Office на этом компьютере?

U vas jehst' pa-K'EHT Office na EH-təm kam-PJU-tə-rə?

This application won't install on my device.
Это приложение не устанавливается на моём устройстве.
EH-tə pr'i-la-ZHEH-n'i-jeh n'eh us-ta-NAV-l'i-va-jeh-tsa na ma-JOM us-TROJ-stv'eh.

Can you change the channel on the television?
Вы можете переключить канал?
Vy MO-zheh-t'eh p'eh-r'eh-kl'u-CHIT' ka-NAL?

I think a fuse blew.
Кажется, взорвался предохранитель.
KA-zheh-tsa, vzar-VAL-s'a pr'eh-da-hra-N'I-t'ehl'.

The screen is black and won't come on.
Экран чёрный и не загорается.
Ehk-RAN CH'OR-nyj i n'eh za-ga-RA-jeh-tsa.

I keep getting pop-ups on every website.
У меня на всех сайтах появляются всплывающие окна.
U m'eh-N'A na fseh SAJ-tah pa-yav-l'a-JU-tsa fsply-VA-ju-schi-jeh OK-na.

This computer is moving much slower than it should.
Этот компьютер работает намного медленнее, чем должен.
EH-təT kam-PJU-tər ra-BO-ta-jeht nam-NO-gə M'EHD-l'ehn-n'eh-jeh ch'ehm DOL-zhehn.

I need to reactivate my copy of Windows.
Мне нужно обновить свою версию Windows.
Mn'ej NU-zhnə ab-na-V'IT' sva-JU V'EH-r-s'i-ju Windows.

Why is this website blocked on my laptop?
Почему этот сайт заблокирован на моём ноутбуке?
Pa-cheh-MU EH-tət sajt zab-la-K'I-rə-vən na ma-JOM no-ut-BU-k'eh?

Can you show me how to download videos to my computer?
Вы можете показать мне, как скачать видео на мой компьютер?
Vy MO-zheh-t'eh pa-ka-ZAT' mn'eh, kak ska-CHAT' V'I-d'eh-o na moj kam-PJU-tər?

Can I insert a flash drive into this computer?
Я могу вставить флешку в этот компьютер?
Ja ma-GU FSTA-v'it' FLESH-ku v EH-tət kam-PJU-tər?

I want to change computers.

Я хочу сменить компьютер.

Ja ha-CHU sm'eh-N'IT' kam-PJU-tər.

Is Chrome the only browser I can use with this computer?

Chrome это единственный браузер, который я могу использовать на этом компьютере?

Chrome EH-tə jeh-D'IN-stv'eh-nyj BRA-u-z'ehr, ka-TO-ryj ja ma-GU is-POL'-zə-vət' na EH-təm kam-PJU-tə-rə?

Do you track my usage on any of these devices?

Вы отслеживаете мои действия на этих устройствах?

Vy at-SL'EH-zhy-va-j'eh-t'eh ma-I D'EHJ-stv'i-ja na EH-t'ih us-TROJ-stvəh?

CONVERSATION TIPS

Pardon me.
Извините.
Iz-v'i-N'I-t'eh.

Please speak more slowly.
Пожалуйста, говорите медленнее.
Pa-ZHA-ləs-tə, ga-va-R'I-t'eh M'EH-dl'eh-n'eh-jeh.

I don't understand.
Я не понимаю.
Ja n'eh pa-n'i-MA-ju.

Can you say that more clearly?
Не могли бы вы сказать это более разборчиво?
N'eh mag-L'I by vy ska-ZAT' EH-tə BO-l'eh-jeh raz-BOR-ch'eh-və?

I don't speak Russian very well.
Я плохо говорю по-русски.
Ja PLO-hə ga-va-R'U pa-RU-sk'i.

Can you please translate that to English for me?
Не могли бы вы перевести мне это на английский?
N'eh mag-L'I by vy p'eh-r'eh-v'ehs-T'I mn'eh EH-tə na an-GL'I-sk'i-j?

Let's talk over there where it is quieter.
Давайте поговорим там, где не так шумно.
Da-VAJ-t'eh pa-ga-va-R'IM tam, gd'eh n'eh tak SHUM-nə.

Sit down over there.
Садитесь сюда.
Sa-D'I-t'ehs' s'u-DA.

May I?
Можно?
MOZH-nə?

I am from America.
Я из Америки.
Ja iz a-M'EH-r'i-k'i.

Am I talking too much?
Я слишком много говорю?
Ja SL'I-shkəm MNO-gə ga-va-R'U?

I speak your language badly.
Я плохо говорю на вашем языке.
Ja PLO-hə ga-va-R'U na VA-shehm jə-zy-K'EH.

Am I saying that word correctly?
Я правильно произношу это слово?
Ja PRA-v'il'-nə pra-iz-na-SHU EH-tə SLO-və?

You speak English very well.
Вы очень хорошо говорите по-английски.
Vy O-ch'ehn' ha-ra-SHO ga-va-R'I-t'eh pa-an-GL'I -sk'i.

This is my first time in your lovely country.
Я впервые в вашей замечательной стране.
Ja fp'ehr-VY-jeh v VA-shehj za-m'eh-CHA-t'ehl-nəj stra-N'EH.

Write that information down on this piece of paper.
Напишите мне эту информацию на этом листочке бумаги.
Na-p'i-SHY-t'eh mn'eh EH-tu in-far-MA-tsy-ju na EH-təm l'is-TOCH-k'eh bu-MA-g'i.

Do you understand?
Вы понимаете?
Vy pa-n'i-MA-j'eh-t'eh?

How do you pronounce that word?
Как произносится это слово?
Kak pra-iz-NO-s'i-tsa EH-tə SLO-və?

Is this how you write this word?
Это слово пишется так?
EH-tə SLO-və P'I-sheh-tsa tak?

Can you give me an example?
Вы можете привести мне пример?
Vy MO-zheh-t'eh pr'i-v'ehs-T'I mn'eh pr'i-M'EHR?

Wait a moment, please.

Подождите минутку, пожалуйста.

Pa-dazh-D'I-t'eh m'i-NUT-ku, pa-ZHA-ləs-tə.

If there is anything you want, tell me.

Если вам что-то нужно, скажите мне.

JEH-sl'I vam SHTO-tə NUZH-nə, ska-ZHY-t'eh mn'eh.

I don't want to bother you anymore, so I will go.

Не хочу больше беспокоить вас, так что я пойду.

N'eh ha-CHU BOL'-sheh b'ehs-pa-KO-it' vas, tak shto ja PAJ-du.

Please take care of yourself.

Пожалуйста, берегите себя.

Pa-ZHA-ləs-tə, b'eh-r'eh-G'I-t'eh s'eh-B'A.

When you arrive, let us know.

Сообщите нам, когда приедете.

Sa-ap-SCH'I-t'eh nam, kag-DA pr'i-JEH-d'eh-t'eh.

DATE NIGHT

What is your telephone number?

Какой у вас номер телефона?

Ka-KOJ u vas NO-m'ehr t'eh-l'eh-FO-na?

I'll call you for the next date.

Я позвоню тебе, чтобы назначить следующее свидание.

Ja paz-va-N'U t'eh-B'EH, SHTO-by naz-NA-ch'it' SL'EH-du-sch'eh-jeh sv'i-DA-n'i-jeh.

I had a good time, can't wait to see you again.

Я отлично провёл/провела время, хочу скорее увидеть тебя снова.

Ja at-L'ICH-nə pra-V'OL/pra-v'eh-LA VR'EH-m'a, ha-CHU sko-R'EH-jeh u-V'I'-d'eht' t'eh-B'A SNO-va.

I'll pay for dinner tonight.

Сегодня я плачу за ужин.

S'eh-VOD-n'a ja pla-CHU za U-zhyn.

Dinner at my place?

Поужинаем у меня?

Pa-U-zhy-na-jehm u m'eh-N'A?

I don't think we should see each other anymore.

Думаю, нам не стоит больше видеться.

DU-ma-ju, nam n'eh STO-it BOL'-sheh V'I-d'eh-tsa.

I'm afraid this will be the last time we see each other.

Боюсь, мы увидимся в последний раз.

Ba-JUS', my u-V'I-d'im-s'a f pas-L'EHD-n'ij ras.

You look fantastic.

Ты потрясающе выглядишь.

Ty pat-r'a-SA-ju-sch'eh VYG-l'a-d'ish.

Would you like to dance with me?

Не хочешь потанцевать со мной?

N'eh HO-chehsh pa-tan-ts'eh-VAT' sa mnoj?

Are there any 3D cinemas in this city?

В этом городе есть 3D-кинотеатры?

V EH-tәm GO-rә-de jehst' tr'i-DEH k'i-na-t'eh-AT-ry?

We should walk along the beach.

Мы должны прогуляться по пляжу.

My dal-ZHNY pra-gu-L'A-tsa pa PL'A-zhu.

I hope you like my car.

Надеюсь, тебе нравится моя машина.

Na-D'EH-jus' t'eh-B'EH NRA-v'i-tsa ma-JA ma-SHY-na.

What movies are playing today?

Какие фильмы сегодня показывают?

Ka-K'I-jeh FIL'-my s'eh-VOD-n'a pa-KA-zy-va-jut?

I've seen this film, but I wouldn't mind watching it again.

Я смотрел/смотрела этот фильм, но не против посмотреть его ещё раз.

Ja smat-R'EHL/smat-R'EH-la EH-tәt fil'm, no n'eh PRO-t'if pas-mat-R'EHT' jeh-VO jeh-SCH'O ras.

Do you know how to do the salsa?

Ты умеешь танцевать сальсу?

Ty u-M'EH-jehsh tan-tseh-VAT' SAL'-su?

We can dance all night.

Мы можем танцевать всю ночь.

My MO-zhehm tan-tseh-VAT' fs'u noch.

I have some friends that will be joining us tonight.

Несколько моих друзей присоединятся к нам сегодня.

N'EHS-kal'-kә ma-IH dru-Z'EHJ pr'i-sa-jeh-d'i-N'A-tsa k nam s'eh-VOD-n'a.

Is this a musical or a regular concert?

Это мюзикл или обычный концерт?

EH-tә M'U-z'ikl I-l'i a-BYCH-nyj kan-TSEHRT?

Did you get VIP tickets?

У тебя VIP билеты?

U t'eh-B'A v'ip bi-L'E-ty?

I'm going to have to cancel on you tonight. Maybe another time?
Мне придётся отменить наше свидание сегодня. Может, в другой раз?
Mn'eh pri-DYOT-sya at-m'eh-N'IT' NA-sheh svi-DA-n'i-jeh se-VOD-nya. MO-zheht v dru-GOJ ras?

If you want, we can go to your place.
Если хочешь, мы можем пойти к тебе.
JEH-sl'I HO-chehsh, my MO-zhehm paj-T'I k t'eh-B'EH.

I'll pick you up tonight.
Я заеду за тобой сегодня вечером.
Ja za-JEH-du za ta-BOJ s'eh-VOD-n'a V'EH-cheh-rəm.

This one is for you!
Это тебе!
EH-tə t'eh-B'EH!

What time does the party start?
Во сколько начинается вечеринка?
Va SKOL'-kə na-chi-NA-jeh-tsa v'eh-ch'eh-R'IN-ka?

Will it end on time or will you have to leave early?
Мероприятие закончится вовремя, или тебе придётся уйти раньше?
M'eh-ra-p'ri-JA-t'i-jeh za-KON-ch'i-tsa VO-vr'eh-m'a, I-l'I t'eh-B'EH pr'i-D'O-tsa uj-T'I RA-n'sheh?

Did you like your gift?
Тебе понравился подарок?
T'eh-B'EH pan-RA-v'il-s'a pa-DA-rək?

I want to invite you to watch a movie with me tonight.
Я хочу пригласить тебя посмотреть со мной фильм сегодня.
Ja ha-CHU pr'i-gla-S'IT' t'eh-B'A pas-mat-R'EHT' sa mnoj fil'm s'eh-VO-dn'a.

Do you want anything to drink?
Хочешь чего-нибудь выпить?
HO-chehsh ch'eh-VO-n'i-but' VY-pit'?

I am twenty-six years old.
Мне двадцать шесть лет.
Mn'eh DVA-tsat' shehst' l'eht.

You're invited to a small party I'm having at my house.
Я приглашаю тебя на небольшую вечеринку у меня дома.
Ja pr'ig-la-SHA-ju t'eh-B'A na n'eh-bal'-SHU-ju v'eh-cheh-R'IN-ku y m'eh-N'A DO-ma.

I love you.
Я тебя люблю.
Ja t'eh-B'A l'ub-L'U.

We should go to the arcade.
Давай пойдём поиграем на игровых автоматах.
Da-VAJ paj-D'OM pa-ig-RA-jehm na ig-ra-VYH af-ta-MA-tah.

Have you ever played this game before?
Ты раньше играл/играла в эту игру?
Ty RAN'-sheh ig-RAL/ig-RA-la v EH-tu ig-RU?

Going on this ferry would be really romantic.
Было бы очень романтично прокатиться на этом пароме.
BY-lə by O-chehn' ra-man-T'ICH-nə pra-ka-T'I-tsa na EH-təm pa-RO-m'eh.

How about a candlelight dinner?
Как насчёт ужина при свечах?
Kak nas-CH'OT U-zhy-na pr'i sv'eh-CHAH?

Let's dance and sing!
Давай танцевать и петь!
Da-VAJ tan-tseh-VAT' i p'eht'!

Will you marry me?
Ты выйдешь за меня замуж?
Ty VYJ-d'ehsh za m'eh-N'A ZA-mush?

Set the table, please.
Накрой на стол, пожалуйста.
Nak-ROJ na stol, pa-ZHA-ləs-tə.

Here are the dishes and the glasses.
Вот тарелки и бокалы.
Vot ta-R'EHL-k'i i ba-KA-ly.

Where is the cutlery?
Где приборы?
Gd'eh pr'i-BO-ry?

May I hold your hand?

Могу я взять тебя за руку?

Ma-GU ja vz'at' t'eh-B'A za RU-ku?

Let me get that for you.

Позволь мне помочь.

Paz-VOL' mn'eh pa-MOCH.

I think our song is playing!

Кажется, наша песня играет.

KA-zheh-tsa NA-sha P'EHS-n'a ig-RA-jeht.

Let's make a wish together.

Давай загадаем желание вместе.

Da-VAJ za-ga-DA-jehm zheh-LA-n'i-jeh VM'EHS-t'eh.

Is there anything that you want from me?

Тебе что-нибудь нужно?

T'eh-B'EH SHTO-n'i-but' NUZH-nə?

There is nowhere I would rather be than right here with you.

Нет места лучше, чем здесь, с тобой.

N'eht M'EHS-ta LU-chsheh, chehm zd'ehs' s ta-BOJ.

I'll give you a ride back to your place.

Я подвезу тебя до дома.

Ja pad-v'eh-ZU t'eh-B'A da DO-ma.

Would you like me to hold your purse?

Может, мне подержать твою сумочку?

MO-zheht mn'eh pa-d'ehr-ZHAT' tva-JU SU-məch-ku?

Let's pray before we eat our meal.

Давай помолимся перед едой.

Da-VAJ pa-MO-l'im-s'a P'EH-r'ehd jeh-DOJ.

Do you need a napkin?

Тебе нужна салфетка?

T'eh-B'EH nuzh-NA sal-F'EHT-ka?

I'm thirsty.

Я хочу пить.

Ja ha-CHU p'it'.

I hope you enjoy your meal.

Надеюсь, тебе нравится еда.

Na-D'EH-jus' t'eh-B'EH NRA-v't-tsa jeh-DA.

I need to add more salt to the saltshaker.

Мне нужно добавить соли в солонку.

Mn'eh NUZH-nə da-BA-v'it' SO-l'i f sa-LON-ku.

We should get married!

Давай поженимся!

Da-VAJ pa-ZHEH-n'i-ms'a.

How old are you?

Сколько тебе лет?

SKOL'-kə t'eh-B'EH l'eht?

Will you dream of me?

Ты будешь мечтать обо мне?

Ty BU-d'ehsh m'ehch-TAT' A-bə mn'EH?

Thank you very much for the wonderful date last night.

Большое спасибо за прекрасное свидание вчера.

Bal'-SHO-jeh spa-S'I-bə za pr'eh-KRAS-n'eh-jeh sv'i-DA-ni-jeh vch'eh-RA.

Would you like to come to a party this weekend?

Хочешь пойти на вечеринку на этих выходных?

HO-chehsh paj-T'I na v'eh-ch'eh-R'IN-ku na EH-t'ih vy-hə-DNYH?

This Saturday night, right?

В эту субботу вечером, верно?

V EH-tu su-BO-tu V'EH-ch'eh-rəm, V'EHR-nə?

I will be lonely without you.

Мне будет одиноко без тебя.

Mn'eh BU-d'eht a-d'i-NO-kə b'ehs t'eh-B'A.

Please stay the night?

Пожалуйста, останься на ночь.

Pa-ZHA-lə-stə, as-TAN'-s'a NA nəch.

I like your fragrance.

Мне нравится твой аромат.

Mn'eh NRA-v'i-tsa tvoj a-ra-MAT.

That is a beautiful outfit you're wearing.

Ты очень красиво одет/одета.

Ty O-ch'ehn' kra-S'I-və a-D'EHT/a-D'EH-ta.

You look beautiful.

Ты прекрасно выглядишь.

Ty pr'ehk-RAS-nə VYG-l'a-d'ish.

Let me help you out of the car.

Позволь мне помочь тебе выйти из машины.

Paz-VOL' mn'eh pa-MOCH t'eh-B'EH VYJ-t'i iz ma-SHY-ny.

Sarah, will you come with me to dinner?

Сара, ты пойдёшь поужинать со мной?

SA-ra, ty paj-D'OSH pa-U-zhy-nat' sa mnoj?

I would like to ask you out on a date.

Я бы хотел/хотела пригласить тебя на свидание.

Ja by ha-T'EHL/ha-T'EH-la pr'ig-la-S'IT' t'eh-B'A na sv'i-DA-n'i-jeh.

Are you free tonight?

Ты свободен/свободна сегодня?

Ty sva-BO-d'ehn/sva-BOD-na s'eh-VOD-n'a?

This is my phone number. Call me anytime.

Это мой номер телефона. Звони мне в любое время.

EH-tə moj NO-m'ehr t'eh-l'eh-FO-na. Zva-N'I mn'eh v l'u-BO-jeh VR'EH-m'a.

Can I hug you?

Можно тебя обнять?

MOZH-nə t'eh-B'A ab-N'AT'?

Would you like to sing karaoke?

Хочешь спеть в караоке?

HO-chehsh sp'eht' f ka-ra-O-k'eh?

What kind of song would you like to sing?

Какую песню ты хочешь спеть?

Ka-KU-ju P'EHS-n'u ty HO-chehsh sp'eht'?

Have you ever sung this song before?

Ты пел/пела эту песню раньше?

Ty p'ehl/P'EH-la EH-tu P'EHS-n'u RAN'-sheh?

We can sing it together.
Мы можем спеть её вместе.
My MO-zhehm sp'eht' jeh-JO VM'EHS-t'eh.

Can I kiss you?
Можно тебя поцеловать?
MOZH-nə t'eh-B'A pa-ts'eh-la-VAT'?

Are you cold?
Тебе холодно?
T'eh-B'EH HO-lə-dnə?

We can stay out as late as you want.
Мы можем гулять столько, сколько ты захочешь.
My MO-zhehm gu-L'AT' STOL'-kə, SKOL'-kə ty za-HO-chesh.

Please, dinner is on me.
Пожалуйста, я угощаю.
Pa-ZHA-lə-stə, ja u-ga-SCHA-ju.

Shall we split the bill?
Мы разделим счёт?
My raz-D'EH-l'im CH'OT?

We should spend more time together.
Мы должны больше времени проводить вместе.
My dal-ZHNY BOL'-sheh VR'EH-m'eh-n'i pra-va-D'IT' VM'EHS-t'eh.

We should walk the town tonight.
Давай прогуляемся по городу сегодня вечером?
Da-VAJ pra-gu-L'A-jehm-s'a pa GO-rə-du s'eh-VOD-n'a V'EH-ch'eh-rəm?

Did you enjoy everything?
Тебе всё понравилось?
T'eh-B'EH fs'o pan-RA-v'i-ləs'?

MONEY AND SHOPPING

May I try this on?

Можно мне примерить это?

MOZH-nə mn'eh pr'i-M'EH-r'it' EH-tə?

How much does this cost?

Сколько это стоит?

SKOL'-kə EH-tə STO-it?

Do I sign here or here?

Мне расписаться здесь или здесь?

Mn'eh ras-p'i-SA-tsa zd'ehs' I-li zd'ehs'?

Is that your final price?

Это ваша окончательная цена?

EH-tə VA-sha a-kan-CHA-t'ehl'-na-ja tseh-NA?

Where do I find toiletries?

Где я могу найти косметику?

Gd'eh ja ma-GU naj-T'I kas-M'EH-t'i-ku?

Would you be willing to take five dollars for this item?

Вы согласны продать эту вещь за пять долларов?

Vy sag-LAS-ny pra-DAT' EH-tu v'ehsch za p'at' DO-lə-rəf?

I can't afford it at that price.

Я не могу себе позволить такую цену.

Ja n'eh ma-GU paz-VO-l'it' s'eh-B'EH ta-KU-ju tseh-NU.

I can find this cheaper somewhere else.

Я могу найти это дешевле в другом месте.

Ja ma-GU SE-be naj-T'I EH-tə d'eh-SHEH-vl'eh v dru-GOM M'EHS-t'eh.

Is there a way we can haggle on price?

Мы можем договориться о цене?

My MO-zhehm da-ga-va-R'I-tsa a tseh-N'EH?

How many of these have you sold today?
Сколько этого вы продали сегодня?
SKOL'-kə EH-tə-və vy pra-DA-l'i s'eh-VO-dn'a?

Can you wrap that up as a gift?
Вы можете упаковать это в подарочную упаковку?
Vy MO-zheh-t'eh u-pa-ka-VAT' EH-tə f pa-DA-rach-nu-ju u-pa-KOF-ku?

Do you provide personalized letters?
Вы делаете индивидуальную рассылку?
Vy D'EH-la-jeh-t'eh in-d'i-v'i-du-AL'-nu-ju ra-SYL-ku?

I would like this to be special delivered to my hotel.
Я бы хотел/хотела, чтобы это доставили в мой отель.
Ja by ha-T'EHL/ha-T'EH-la, SHTO-by EH-tə das-TA-v'i-l'i v moj a-TEHL'.

Can you help me, please?
Не могли бы вы мне помочь?
N'eh mag-L'I by vy mn'eh pa-MOCH?

We should go shopping at the market.
Давай пойдём за покупками на рынок.
Da-VAJ paj-D'OM za pa-KUP-ka-m'i na RY-nək.

Are you keeping track of the clothes that fit me?
Вы откладываете одежду, которая мне подошла?
Vy at-KLA-dy-va-jeh-t'eh a-D'EH-zhdu, ka-TO-ra-ja mn'eh pa-dash-LA?

Can I have one size up?
Можно мне на один размер больше?
MOZH-nə mn'eh na a-D'IN raz-M'EHR BOL'-sheh?

How many bathrooms does the apartment have?
Сколько в этой квартире санузлов?
SKOL'-kə v EH-təj kvar-T'I-r'eh san-uz-LOF?

Where's the kitchen?
Где кухня?
Gd'eh KUH-n'a?

Does this apartment have a gas or electric stove?
В этой квартире газовая или электрическая плита?
V EH-təj kvar-T'I-r'eh GA-zə-va-ja I-l'i eh-l'ehk-TR'I-chehs-ka-ja pl'i-TA?

Is there a spacious backyard?
Там есть просторный задний двор?
Tam jehst' pras-TOR-nyj ZAD-n'ij dvor?

How much is the down payment?
Какой будет задаток?
Ka-KOJ BU-d'eht za-DA-tək?

I'm looking for a furnished apartment.
Я ищу квартиру с мебелью.
Ja i-SCH'U kvar-T'I-ru s M'EH-b'ehl'-ju.

I need a two-bedroom apartment to rent.
Я хочу снять двухкомнатную квартиру.
Ja ha-CHU sn'at' dvuh-KOM-nat-nə-ju kvar-T'I-ru.

I'm looking for an apartment with utilities paid.
Я ищу квартиру, в оплату которой входит оплата коммунальных
услуг.
Ja i-SCH'U kvar-T'I-ru, v ap-LA-tu ka-TO-rəj FHO-d'it ap-LA-ta ka-mu-NAL'-nyh us-LUK.

The carpet in this apartment needs to be pulled up.
Ковер в этой квартире нужно убрать.
Ka-V'OR v EH-təj kvar-T'I-r'eh NUZH-nə ub-RAT'.

I need you to come down on the price of this apartment.
Мне нужно, чтобы вы снизили цену за эту квартиру.
Mn'eh NUZH-nə, SHTO-by vy SN'I-z'i-l'i TSEH-nu za EH-tu kvar-T'I-ru.

Will I be sharing this place with other people?
Я буду жить здесь вместе с другими людьми?
Ja BU-du zhyt' zd'ehs' VM'ES-t'eh z dru-G'I-m'i l'ud'-M'I?

How do you work the fireplace?
Как работает камин?
Kak ra-BO-ta-jeht ka-M'IN?

Are there any curfew rules attached to this apartment?
Для этой квартиры существует комендантский час?
Dl'a EH-təj kvar-T'I-ry su-scheh-STVU-jeht ka-m'ehn-DAN-sk'ij chas?

How long is the lease for this place?
На сколько сдаётся эта квартира?
Na SKOL'-kə zda-JO-tsa EH-tə kvar-T'I-ra?

Do you gamble?

Ты любишь азартные игры?

Ty L'U-b'ish a-ZAR-tny-jeh IG-ry?

We should go to a casino.

Давай сходим в казино.

Da-VAJ SHO-d'im f ka-z'i-NO.

There is really good horse racing in this area.

В этом районе проводятся очень хорошие скачки.

V EH-təm ra-JO-n'eh pra-VO-d'a-tsa O-chehn' ha-RO-shy-jeh SKACH-k'i.

Do you have your ID so that we can go gambling?

У тебя есть удостоверение личности, чтобы мы могли пойти играть в азартные игры?

U t'eh-B'A jehst' u-das-ta-v'eh-R'EH-n'i-jeh L'ICH-nas-t'i, SHTO-by my mag-L'I paj-T'I ig-RAT' v a-ZAR-tny-jeh I-gry?

Who did you bet on?

На кого ты поставил/поставила?

Na ka-VO ty pas-TA-v'il/pas-TA-v'i-la?

I am calling about the apartment that you placed in the ad.

Я звоню по объявлению о квартире.

Ja zva-N'U pa ab-jav-L'EH-n'i-ju o kvar-T'I-r'eh.

How much did you bet?

Сколько ты поставил/поставила?

SKOL'-kə ty pas-TA-v'il/pas-TA-v'i-la?

We should go running with the bulls!

Мы должны побегать с быками!

My dalzh-NY pa-B'EH-gat' s by-KA-m'i!

Is Adele coming to sing at this venue tonight?

Адель будет петь здесь сегодня вечером?

A-dehl' BU-d'eht p'eht' zd'ehs' s'eh-VOD-n'a V'EH-ch'eh-rəm?

How much is the item you have in the window?

Сколько стоит эта вещь у вас на витрине?

SKOL'-kə STO-it EH-tə v'ehsch u vas na v'it-R'I-n'eh?

Do you have payment plans?

Вы продаёте в рассрочку?

Vy pra-da-JO-t'eh v ras-SROCH-ku?

Do these two items come together?

Эти две вещи продаются вместе?

EH-t'i dv'eh V'EH-schi pra-da-JU-tsa VM'EHS-t'eh?

Are these parts cheaply made?

Это дешёвые варианты запчастей?

EH-tə d'eh-SHO-vy-jeh va-r'i-AN-ty zap-chas-T'EHJ?

This is a huge bargain!

Это огромная скидка!

Eh-H-tə ag-ROM-na-ja SK'IT-ka!

I like this. How does three hundred dollars sound?

Мне это нравится. Как насчёт трёхсот долларов?

Mn'eh EH-tə NRA-v'i-tsa. Kak nas-CH'OT tr'oh-SOT DO-lə-rəf?

Two hundred is all I can offer. That is my final price.

Двести — это всё, что я могу предложить. Это моя окончательная цена.

DV'EHS-t'i — EH-tə fs'o, shto ja ma-GU pr'ehd-la-ZHYT'. EH-tə ma-JA a-kan-CHA-t'ehl'-na-ja tseh-NA.

Do you have cheaper versions of this item?

У вас есть более дешёвые варианты этого товара?

U vas jehst' BO-l'eh-jeh d'eh-SHO-vy-jeh va-r'i-AN-ty EH-tə-və ta-VA-ra?

Do you have the same item with a different pattern?

У вас есть такая же вещь, но с другим узором?

U vas jehst' ta-KA-ja zheh v'ehsch, no z dru-G'IM u-ZO-rəm?

How much is this worth?

Сколько это стоит?

SKOL'-kə EH-tə STO-it?

Can you pack this up and send it to my address on file?

Вы можете упаковать это и отправить по указанному адресу?

Vy MO-zheh-t'eh u-pa-ka-VAT' EH-tə i at-PRA-v'it' pa u-KA-zə-nə-mu A-dr'eh-su?

Does it fit?

Размер подходит?

Raz-M'EHR pad-HO-d'it?

They are too big for me.
Они мне велики.
A-n'i mn'eh v'eh-l'i-K'I.

Please find me another but in the same size.
Пожалуйста, найдите мне другую вещь, но такого же размера.
Pa-ZHA-ləs-tə, naj-D'I-t'eh mn'eh dru-GU-ju v'ehsch, no ta-KO-və zheh raz-M'EH-ra.

It fits, but is tight around my waist.
Размер подходит, но в талии тесновато.
Raz-M'EHR pad-HO-d'it, no f TA-l'i-i t'ehs-na-VA-tə.

Can I have one size down?
Можно мне на один размер меньше?
MOZH-nə mn'eh na a-D'IN raz-M'EHR M'EHN'-sheh?

Size twenty, American.
Двадцатый размер, американский.
Dva-TSA-tyj raz-M'EHR, a-m'eh-r'i-KAN-skij.

Do you sell appliances for the home?
Вы продаёте бытовую технику?
Vy pra-da-JO-t'eh by-ta-VU-ju T'EH-hn'i-ku?

Not now, thank you.
Не сейчас, спасибо.
N'eh s'eh-CHAS, spa-S'I-bə.

I'm looking for something special.
Я ищу что-то особенное.
Ja i-SCH'U SHTO-tə a-SO-b'ehn-na-jeh.

I'll call you when I need you.
Я позову вас, когда мне будет нужно.
Ja pa-za-VU vas, kag-DA mn'eh BU-d'eht NUZH-nə.

Do you have this in my size?
У вас есть эта вещь моего размера?
U vas jehst' EH-tə v'ehsch ma-jeh-VO raz-m'eh-ra?

On which floor can I find cologne?
На каком этаже я могу найти одеколоны?
Na ka-KOM eh-TA-zheh ja ma-GU naj-T'I a-d'eh-ka-LO-ny?

Where is the entrance?

Где находится вход?

Gd'eh na-HO-d'i-tsa fhod?

Do I exit from that door?

Я смогу выйти через эту дверь?

Ja sma-GU VYJ-t'i CH'EH-r'ehz EH-tu dv'ehr'?

Where is the elevator?

Где находится лифт?

Gd'eh na-HO-d'i-tsa l'ift?

Do I push or pull to get this door open?

Дверь открывается на себя или от себя?

Dv'ehr' at-kry-VA-jeh-tsa NA s'eh-B'A I-l'i at s'eh-B'A?

I already have that, thanks.

У меня это уже есть, спасибо.

U m'eh-N'A EH-tə u-ZHEH jehst', spa-S'I-bə.

Where can I try this on?

Где я могу это примерить?

Gd'eh ja ma-GU EH-tə pr'i-M'EH-r'it'?

This mattress is very soft.

Этот матрас очень мягкий.

EH-tət mat-RAS O-ch'ehn' M'AH-k'ij.

What is a good place for birthday gifts?

Где можно купить хороший подарок на день рождения?

Gd'eh MOZH-nə ku-P'IT' ha-RO-shyj pa-DA-rək na d'ehn' razh-D'EH-n'i-ja?

I'm just looking, but thank you.

Я просто смотрю, но спасибо вам.

Ja PROS-tə sma-TR'U, no spa-S'I-bə vam.

Yes, I will call you when I need you, thank you.

Да, я позову вас, когда вы мне понадобитесь, спасибо.

Da, ja pa-za-VU vas, kag-DA vy mn'eh pa-NA-də-b'i-t'ehs', spa-S'I-bə.

Do you accept returns?

Вы принимаете возвраты?

Vy pr'i-n'i-MA-j'eh-t'eh vaz-VRA-ty?

Here is my card and receipt for the return.

Вот моя карточка и чек для возврата.

Vot ma-JA KAR-tach-ka i ch'ehk dl'a vaz-VRA-ta.

Where are the ladies' clothes?

Где женская одежда?

Gd'eh ZHEN-ska-ja a-D'EHZH-da?

What sizes are available for this item?

В каких размерах у вас есть эта вещь?

F ka-K'IH raz-M'EH-rah u vas jehst' EH-tə v'ehsch?

Is there an ATM machine nearby?

Здесь рядом есть банкомат?

Zd'ehs' R'A-dəm jehst' ban-ka-MAT?

What forms of payment do you accept?

Какие способы оплаты вы принимаете?

Ka-K'I-jeh SPO-sə-by ap-LA-ty vy pr'i-n'i-MA-j'eh-t'eh?

That doesn't interest me.

Меня это не интересует.

M'eh-N'A EH-tə n'eh in-t'eh-r'eh-SU-jeht.

I don't like it, but thank you.

Мне это не нравится, но спасибо.

Mn'eh EH-tə n'eh NRA-v'i-tsa, no spa-S'I-bə.

Do you take American dollars?

Вы принимаете американские доллары?

Vy pr'i-n'i-MA-j'eh-t'eh a-m'eh-r'i-KAN-sk'i-jeh DO-lə-ry?

Can you make change for me?

Вы сможете дать мне сдачу?

Vy SMO-zheh-t'eh dat' mn'eh ZDA-chu?

What is the closest place to get change for my money?

Где находится ближайшее место, где я могу разменять деньги?

G'deh na-HO-d'i-tsa bl'i-ZHAJ-sheh-jeh M'EH-stə, gd'eh ja ma-GU raz-m'eh-N'AT' D'EN-n'g'i?

Are travelers checks able to be changed here?

Здесь можно обменять дорожные чеки?

Zd'ehs' MOZH-nə ab-m'eh-N'AT' da-ROZH-ny-jeh CHEH-k'i?

What is the current exchange rate?
Какой сейчас курс?
Ka-KOJ s'eh-CHAS kurs?

What is the closest place to exchange money?
Где ближайший пункт обмена валюты?
Gd'eh bl'i-ZHAJ-shyj punkt ab-M'EH-na va-L'U-ty?

Do you need to borrow money? How much?
Вам нужно одолжить денег? Сколько?
Vam NUZH-nə a-dal-ZHYT' D'EH-n'ehg? SKOL'-kə?

Can this bank exchange my money?
Я смогу обменять деньги в этом банке?
Ja sma-GU ab-m'eh-N'AT' D'EHN'-g'i v EH-təm BAN-k'eh?

What is the exchange rate for the American dollar?
Какой обменный курс американского доллара?
Ka-KOJ ab-M'EHN-nyj kurs a-m'eh-r'i-KAN-skə-və DO-lə-rə?

Will you please exchange me fifty dollars?
Вы не могли бы обменять мне пятьдесят долларов?
Vy n'eh mag-L'I by ab-m'eh-N'AT' mn'eh p'at'-d'eh-S'AT DO-lə-rəf?

I would like a receipt with that.
Я бы хотел/хотела получить чек за этот товар.
Ja by ha-T'EHL/ha-T'EH-la pa-lu-CHIT' chehk za EH-tət ta-VAR.

Your commission rate is too high.
Ваша комиссия слишком высока.
VA-sha ka-M'I-s'i-ja SL'ISH-kəm vy-sa-KA.

Does this bank have a lower commission rate?
В этом банке более низкая комиссия?
V EH-təm BAN-k'eh BO-l'eh-jeh N'IS-ka-ja ka-M'I-s'i-ja?

Do you take cash?
Вы принимаете наличные?
Vy pr'i-n'i-MA-j'eh-t'eh na-L'ICH-ny-jeh?

Where can I exchange dollars?
Где я могу обменять доллары?
Gd'eh ja ma-GU ab-m'eh-N'AT' DO-lə-ry?

I want to exchange dollars for yen.

Я хочу обменять доллары на йены.

Ja ha-CHU ab-m'eh-N'AT' DO-lə-ry na JEH-ny.

Do you take credit cards?

Вы принимаете кредитные карты?

Vy pr'i-n'i-MA-j'eh-t'eh kr'eh-D'IT-ny-jeh KAR-ty?

Here is my credit card.

Вот моя кредитная карточка.

Vot ma-JA kr'eh-D'IT-na-ja KAR-təch-ka.

One moment, let me check the receipt.

Минуточку, дайте я проверю чек.

Mi-NU-təch-ku, DAJ-t'eh ja pra-V'EH-r'u chehk.

Do I need to pay tax?

Мне нужно платить налог?

Mn'eh NUZH-nə pla-T'IT' na-LOG?

How much is this item with tax?

Сколько это стоит с налогом?

SKOL'-kə EH-tə STO-it s na-LO-gəm?

Where is the cashier?

Где кассир?

Gd'eh ka-S'IR?

Excuse me, I'm looking for a dress.

Извините, я ищу платье.

Iz-v'i-N'I-t'eh, ja i-SCH'U PLAT'-jeh.

That's a lot for that dress.

Это много за это платье.

EH-tə MNO-gə za EH-tə PLAT'-jeh.

Sorry, but I don't want it.

Извините, но я это не хочу.

Iz-v'i-N'I-t'eh, no ja EH-tə n'eh ha-CHU.

Okay I will take it.

Хорошо, я беру это.

Ha-rə-SHO, ja b'eh-RU EH-tə.

I'm not interested if you are going to sell it at that price.

Если вы продаёте это по такой цене, то мне не интересно.

JEH-sl'I vy pra-da-JO-t'eh EH-tə pa TA-koj tseh-N'EH, to mn'eh n'eh in-t'eh-R'EHS-nə.

You are cheating me at the current price.

Такая цена — это обман.

Ta-KA-ja ts'eh-NA — EH-tə ab-MAN.

No thanks. I'll only take it if you lower the price by half.

Нет, спасибо. Я возьму это, только если вы снизите цену наполовину.

N'eht, spa-S'I-bə. Ja vaz'-MU EH-tə TOL'-kə JEH-sl'I vy SN'I-z'i-t'eh TSEH-nu na-pa-la-V'I-nu.

That is a good price, I'll take it.

Это хорошая цена, я беру.

EH-tə ha-RO-sha-ja tseh-NA, ja b'eh-RU.

Do you sell souvenirs for tourists?

Вы продаете сувениры для туристов?

Vy pra-da-JO-t'eh su-v'eh-N'I-ry dl'a tu-R'IS-təf?

Can I have a bag for that?

Можно мне пакет для этого?

MOZH-nə mn'eh pa-K'EHT dl'a EH-tə-və?

Is this the best bookstore in the city?

Это лучший книжный магазин в городе?

EH-tə LUCH-shyj KN'IZH-nyj ma-ga-Z'IN v GO-rə-de?

I would like to go to a game shop to buy comic books.

Я бы хотел/хотела пойти в магазин игр, чтобы купить комиксы.

Ja by ha-T'EHL/ha-T'EH-la paj-T'I v ma-ga-Z'IN igr, SHTO-by ku-P'IT' KO-m'ik-sy.

Are you able to ship my products overseas?

Вы можете отправить мои покупки за границу?

Vy MO-zheh-t'eh at-PRA-v'it' ma-i pa-KUP-k'i za gra-n'i-tsu?

CHILDREN AND PETS

Which classroom does my child attend?

В каком кабинете занимается мой ребёнок?

F ka-KOM ka-b'i-N'EH-t'eh za-n'i-MA-jeh-tsa moj r'eh-B'O-nək?

Is the report due before the weekend?

Доклад нужно сдать до выходных?

Dak-LAT NUZH-nə zdat' da vy-had-NYH?

I'm waiting for my mom to pick me up.

Я жду маму, чтобы она меня забрала.

Ja zhdu MA-mu, SHTO-by a-NA m'eh-N'A zab-ra-LA.

What time does the school bus run?

Во сколько ходит школьный автобус?

Va SKOL'-kə HO-d'it SHKOL'-nyj af-TO-bus?

I need to see the principal.

Я хочу увидеть директора.

Ja ha-CHU u-V'I-d'eht' d'i-R'EHK-tə-ra.

I would like to report bullying.

Я бы хотел/хотела сообщить об издевательствах.

Ja by ha-T'EHL/ha-T'EH-la sa-ap-SCHIT' ab iz-d'eh-VA-t'ehl'-stvəh.

What are the leash laws in this area?

Здесь можно отпускать собак без поводка?

Zd'ehs' MOZH-nə at-pus-KAT' sa-BAK b'ehs pa-vat-KA?

Please keep your dog away from mine.

Пожалуйста, уберите свою собаку от моей.

Pa-ZHA-ləs-tə, u-b'eh-R'I-t'eh sva-JU sa-BA-ku at ma-JEHJ.

My dog doesn't bite.

Моя собака не кусается.

Ma-JA sa-BA-ka n'eh ku-SA-jeh-tsa.

I am allergic to cat hair.

У меня аллергия на кошачью шерсть.

U m'eh-N'A a-l'ehr-G'I-ja na ka-SHA-ch'ju shehrst'.

Don't leave the door open or the cat will run out!

Не оставляйте дверь открытой, или кошка убежит!

N'eh as-tav-L'AJ-t'eh dv'ehr' at-KRY-taj, I-l'i KOSH-ka u-b'eh-ZHYT!

Have you fed the dogs yet?

Ты уже покормил/покормила собак?

Ty u-ZHEH pa-kar-MI-l/pa-kar-M'I-la sa-BAK?

We need to take the dog to the veterinarian.

Нам нужно отвезти собаку к ветеринару.

Nam NUZH-nə at-v'ehs-T'I sa-BA-ku k v'eh-t'eh-r'i-NA-ru.

Are there any open roster spots on the team?

В команде есть свободные места?

F ka-MAN-d'eh jehst' sva-BOD-ny-jeh m'ehs-TA?

My dog is depressed.

Моя собака грустит.

Ma-JA sa-BA-ka grus-T'IT.

Don't feed the dog table scraps.

Не кормите собаку объедками со стола.

N'eh kar-M'I-t'eh sa-BA-ku ab-JEHT-ka-m'i sa sta-LA.

Don't let the cat climb up on the furniture.

Не разрешай кошке лазать по мебели.

N'eh raz-r'eh-SHAJ KOSH-k'eh LA-zat' pa M'EH-b'eh-l'i.

The dog is not allowed to sleep in the bed with you.

Собаке нельзя спать с тобой в постели.

Sa-BA-k'eh n'ehl'-Z'A spat' s ta-BOJ f pas-T'EH-l'i.

There is dog poop on the floor. Clean it up.

На полу собачьи какашки. Убери их.

Na pa-LU sa-BACH'-ji ka-KASH-k'i. Ub'eh-R'I ih.

When was the last time you took the dog for a walk?

Когда вы в последний раз выгуливали собаку?

Kag-DA vy f pas-L'EHD-n'ij ras vy-GU-l'i-va-l'i sa-BA-ku?

Are you an international student? How long are you attending?
Вы иностранный студент? Вы давно занимаетесь?
Vy inas-TRAN-nyj stu-D'EHNT? Vy dav-NO za-n'i-MA-j'eh-t'ehs'?

Are you a French student?
Вы студент/студентка из Франции?
Vy stu-D'EHNT/stu-D'EHN-tka is FRAN-tsy-i?

I am an American student that is here for the semester.
Я студент/студентка из Америки, я здесь на семестр.
Ja stu-D'EHNT/stu-D'EHNT-ka iz a-m'eh-r'i-k'i, ja zd'ehs' na s'eh-M'EHSTR.

Please memorize this information.
Пожалуйста, запомните эту информацию.
Pa-ZHA-ləs-tə, za-POM-n'i-t'eh EH-tu in-far-MA-tsy-ju.

This is my roommate Max.
Это мой сосед по комнате Макс.
EH-tə moj sa-S'EHD pa KOM-na-t'eh Maks.

Are these questions likely to appear on the exams?
Эти вопросы могут попасться на экзамене?
EH-t'i vap-RO-sy MO-gut pa-PAS-tsa na ehg-ZA-m'eh-n'eh?

Teacher, say that once more, please.
Учитель, повторите, пожалуйста, ещё раз.
U-CHI-t'ehl, paf-ta-R'I-t'eh, pa-ZHA-ləs-tə, jeh-SCH'O ras.

I didn't do well on the quiz.
Я плохо сдал/сдала тест.
Ja PLO-hə zdal/zda-LA tehst.

Go play outside, but stay where I can see you.
Иди поиграй на улице, но будь там, где я могу тебя видеть.
I-D'I pa-ig-RAJ na U-l'i-tseh, no but' tam gd'eh ja ma-GU t'eh-B'A V'I-d'eht'.

How is your daughter?
Как ваша дочь?
Kak VA-sha doch'?

I'm going to walk the dogs.
Я пойду погуляю с собаками.
Ja paj-DU pa-gu-L'A-ju s sa-BA-ka-m'i.

She's not very happy here.
Она не очень счастлива здесь.
A-NA n'eh O-ch'ehn' SCH'AS-l'i-və zd'ehs'.

I passed the quiz with high marks!
Я сдал/сдала тест на хорошую оценку!
Ja zdal/zda-LA tehst na ha-RO-shu-ju a-TSEH-nku!

What program are you enrolled in?
На какой курс ты записан/записана?
Na ka-KOJ kurs ty za-P'I-san/za-P'I-sa-na?

I really like my English teacher.
Мне очень нравится мой учитель/моя учительница английского.
Mn'eh O-chehn' NRA-v'i-tsa moj u-CHI-t'ehl'/ma-JA u-CHI-t'ehl'-n'i-tsa an-GL'I-skə-və.

I have too much homework to do.
У меня очень большое домашнее задание.
U m'eh-N'A O-chehn' bal'-SHO-jeh da-MASH-n'eh-jeh za-DA-n'i-jeh.

Tomorrow, I have to take my dog to the vet.
Завтра мне нужно отвезти мою собаку к ветеринару.
ZAF-trə mn'eh NUZH-nə at-v'ehs-T'I ma-JU sa-BA-ku k v'e-t'eh-r'i-NA-ru.

When do we get to go to lunch?
Во сколько нам нужно идти обедать?
Va SKOL'-kə nam NUZH-nə i-T'I a-B'EH-dat'?

My dog swallowed something he shouldn't have.
Моя собака проглотила что-то лишнее.
Ma-JA sa-BA-ka prag-la-T'I-lə SHTO-tə L'ISH-n'eh-jeh.

We need more toys for our dog to play with.
Нам нужно больше игрушек для нашей собаки.
Nam NUZH-nə BOL'-sheh ig-RU-shehk dl'a NA-shehj sa-BA-k'i.

Can you please change the litter box?
Вы не могли бы поменять мусорный пакет?
Vy n'eh mag-L'I by pa-m'eh-N'AT' MU-sər-nyj pa-K'EHT?

Get a lint brush and roll it to get the hair off your clothes.
Возьми щётку с клейкой лентой, чтобы убрать шерсть с одежды.
Vaz'-M'I SCH'O-tku s KL'EHJ-kəj L'EHN-təj, SHTO-by ub-RAT' shehrst' s a-D'EHZH-dy.

Can you help me study?
Ты можешь помочь мне с учёбой?
Ty MO-zhehsh pa-MOCH mn'eh s u-CH'O-bəj?

I have to go study in my room.
Мне нужно пойти в свою комнату учиться.
Mn'eh NUZH-nə paj-T'I f sva-ju KOM-nətu u-CHI-tsa.

We went to the campus party, and it was a lot of fun.
Мы ходили на вечеринку в студгородке, было очень весело.
My ha-D'I-l'i na v'eh-ch'eh-R'IN-ku f stud-ga-rat-K'EH, BY-lə O-chehn'
V'EH'-s'eh-lə.

Can you use that word in a sentence?
Вы не могли бы использовать это слово в предложении?
Vy n'eh mag-L'I by is-POL'-zə-vət' EH-tə SLO-və f pr'ehd-la-ZHEH-n'i-i?

How do you spell that word?
Как пишется это слово?
Kak P'I-sheh-tsa EH-tə SLO-və?

Go play with your brother.
Поиграй со своим братом.
Pa-ig-RAJ sa sva-IM BRA-təm.

Come inside! It is dinnertime.
Домой! Пора ужинать.
Da-MOJ! Pa-RA U-zhy-nat'.

Tell me about your day.
Расскажи, как прошёл твой день.
Ras-ka-ZHY, kak pra-SHOL tvoj d'ehn'.

Is there anywhere you want to go?
Хочешь куда-нибудь пойти?
HO-chehsh ku-DA-n'i-but' paj-T'I?

How are you feeling?
Как ты себя чувствуешь?
Kak ty s'eh-B'A CHUS-tvu-jehsh?

What do you want me to make for dinner tonight?
Что ты хочешь, чтобы я приготовил/приготовила на ужин сегодня
вечером?

Shto ty HO-chehsh, SHTO-by ja pr'i-ga-TO-v'i-l/pr'i-ga-TO-v'i-la na U-zhyn s'eh-VOD-n'a V'EH-cheh-rəm?

It's time for you to take a bath.
Тебе пора идти умываться.
T'eh-B'EH pa-RA i-T'I u-my-VA-tsa.

Brush your teeth and wash behind your ears.
Почисти зубы и помой за ушами.
Pa-CHI-st'i ZU-by i pa-MOJ za u-SHA-m'i.

You're not wearing that to bed.
Нельзя ложиться в этом спать.
NEL'-z'a la-ZHY-tsa v EH-təm spat'.

I don't like the way you're dressed. Put something else on.
Мне не нравится, как ты одет/одета. Надень что-то другое.
Mn'eh n'eh NRA-v'i-tsa, kak ty a-D'EHT/a-D'EH-ta. Na-D'EHN' SHTO-tə dru-GO-jeh.

Did you make any friends today?
Ты сегодня познакомился/познакомилась с кем-нибудь?
Ty s'eh-VOD-n'a paz-na-KO-m'il-s'a/paz-na-KO-m'i-las' s K'EHM-n'i-but'?

Let me see your homework.
Покажи мне свою домашнюю работу.
Pa-ka-ZHY mn'eh sva-JU da-MASH-n'u-ju ra-BO-tu.

Do I need to call your school?
Мне позвонить в школу?
Mn'eh paz-va-N'IT' f SHKO-lu?

The dog can't go outside right now.
Собаке нельзя выйти прямо сейчас.
Sa-BA-k'eh n'ehl'-Z'A VYJ-t'i PR'A-mə s'eh-CHAS.

Is the new quiz going to be available next week?
Новый тест будет готов на следующей неделе?
NO-vyj tehst BU-d'eht ga-TOF na SL'EH-du-schehj n'eh-D'EH-l'eh?

Are we allowed to use calculators with the test?
Можно пользоваться калькуляторами во время теста?
MOZH-nə POL'-zə-və-tsa kal'-ku-L'A-tə-rə-m'i va VR'EH-m'a TEH-sta?

I would like to lead today's lesson.
Я бы хотел/хотела провести сегодняшний урок.
Ja by ha-T'EHL/ha-T'EH-la pra-v'ehs-T'I se-VOD-n'ash-nij u-ROK.

I have a dorm curfew, so I need to go back.
У меня в общежитии комендантский час, так что мне пора возвращаться.
U m'eh-N'A v ap-scheh-ZHY-t'i-i ka-m'ehn-DAN-skij chas, tak shto mn'eh pa-RA vaz-vra-SCHA-tsa.

Do I have to use pencil or ink?
Нужно писать карандашом или ручкой?
NUZH-nə p'i-SAT' ka-ran-da-SHOM I-l'i RUCH-kəj?

Are cell phones allowed in class?
На уроке можно пользоваться мобильным телефоном?
Na u-RO-k'eh MOZH-nə POL'-zə-va-tsa ma-B'IL'-nym t'eh-l'eh-FO-nəm?

Where can I find the nearest dog park?
Где находится ближайший парк для собак?
Gd'eh na-HO-d'i-tsa bl'i-ZHAJ-shyj park dl'a sa-BAK?

Are dogs allowed to be off their leash here?
Здесь можно выгуливать собак без поводка?
Zd'ehs' MOZH-nə vy-GU-l'i-vat' sa-BAK b'ehs pa-vat-KA?

Are children allowed here?
Здесь можно быть с детьми?
Zd'ehs' MOZH-nə byt' z d'eht'-M'I?

I would like to set up a play date with our children.
Я бы хотел/хотела назначить день игр для наших детей.
Ja by ha-T'EHL'/ha-T'EH-la naz-NA-chit' d'ehn' igr dl'a NA-shih d'eh-TEHJ.

I would like to invite you to my child's birthday party.
Я приглашаю вас на день рождения к моему ребёнку.
Ja pr'ig-la-SHA-ju vas na d'ehn' razh-D'EH-n'i-ja k ma-jeh-MU r'eh-B'O-nku.

Did you miss your dorm curfew last night?
Ты вчера не успел/успела вернуться в общежитие до комендантского часа?
Ty vche-RA n'eh us-P'EHL/us-P'EH-la v'ehr-NU-tsa v ap-scheh-ZHY-ti-jeh da ka-m'ehn-DAN-skə-və CHA-sa?

117

TRAVELER'S GUIDE

Over there is the library.
Библиотека вон там.
B'i-bl'i-a-T'EH-ka von tam.

Just over there.
Вон там.
Von tam.

Yes, this way.
Да, сюда.
Da, s'u-DA.

I haven't done anything wrong.
Я не сделал/сделала ничего плохого.
Ja n'eh ZD'EH-lal/ZD'EH-la-la n'i-cheh-VO pla-HO-və.

It was a misunderstanding.
Произошло недопонимание.
Pra-i-zash-LO n'eh-da-pa-n'i-MA-n'i-jeh.

I am an American citizen.
Я гражданин/гражданка США.
Ja grazh-da-N'IN/grazh-DAN-ka seh-sheh-A.

We are tourists on vacation.
Мы туристы на отдыхе.
My tu-R'IS-ty na OD-dy-h'eh.

I am looking for an apartment.
Я ищу квартиру.
Ja i-SCH'U kvar-T'I-ru.

This is a short-term stay.
Это для недолгого пребывания.
EH-tə dl'a n'eh-DOL-gə-və pr'eh-by-VA-n'i-ja.

I am looking for a place to rent.
Я хочу снять жильё.
Ja ha-CHU sn'at' zhyl'-JO.

Where can we grab a quick bite to eat?
Где можно быстро перекусить?
Gd'eh MOZH-nə BYS-trə p'eh-r'eh-ku-S'IT'?

We need the cheapest place you can find.
Нам нужно самое дешёвое место, которое вы можете найти.
Nam NUZH-nə SA-mə-jeh d'eh-SHO-və-jeh M'EHS-tə, ka-TO-rə-jeh vy MO-zheh-t'eh naj-T'I.

Do you have a map of the city?
У вас есть карта города?
U vas jehst' KAR-ta GO-rə-da?

What places do tourists usually visit when they come here?
Куда обычно ходят туристы, когда они сюда приезжают?
Ku-DA a-BYCH-nə HO-d'at tu-R'IS-ty, kag-DA a-n'i s'u-DA pr'i-jehz-ZHA-jut?

Can you take our picture, please?
Не могли бы вы сфотографировать нас, пожалуйста?
N'eh mag-L'I by vy sfa-tag-ra-F'I-rə-vat' nas, pa-ZHA-ləs-tə?

Do you take foreign credit cards?
Вы принимаете иностранные кредитные карты?
Vy pri-n'i-MA-j'eh-t'eh i-nas-TRAN-ny-jeh kr'eh-D'IT-ny-jeh KAR-ty?

I would like to rent a bicycle to take us around the city.
Я бы хотел/хотела взять напрокат велосипед, чтобы прокатиться по городу.
Ja by ha-T'EHL/ha-T'EH-la vz'at' na-pra-KAT v'eh-la-s'i-P'EHD, SHTO-by pra-ka-T'I-tsa pa GO-rə-du.

Do you mind if I take pictures here?
Вы не против, если я сделаю здесь фото?
Vy n'eh PRO-t'if, JEH-sl'i ja ZD'EH-la-ju zd'ehs' FO-tə?

ANSWERS

Yes, to some extent.

Да, в некоторой мере.

Da, v N'EH-ka-tə-rə'j M'EH-r'eh.

I'm not sure.

Я не уверен/уверена.

Ja n'eh u-V'EH-r'ehn/u-V'EH-r'eh-na.

Yes, go ahead.

Да, пожалуйста.

Da, pa-ZHA-ləs-tə.

Yes, just like you.

Да, как и вы.

Da, kak i vy.

No, no problem at all.

Нет, вообще никаких проблем.

Net, vap-SCH'EH n'i-ka-K'IH prab-L'EHM.

This is a little more expensive than the other item.

Это немного дороже, чем та другая вещь.

EH-tə n'ehm-NO-gə da-RO-zheh, ch'ehm ta dru-GA-ja v'ehsch.

My city is small but nice.

Мой город небольшой, но хороший.

Moj GO-rəd n'eh-bal'-SHOJ, no ha-RO-shyj.

This city is quite big.

Этот город довольно большой.

EH-tət GO-rəd da-VOL'-nə bal'-SHOJ.

I'm from America.

Я из Америки.

Ja iz a-M'EH-r'i-k'i.

We'll wait for you.
Мы будем вас ждать.
My BU-d'ehm vas zhdat'.

I love going for walks.
Я люблю гулять.
Ja l'ub-L'U gu-L'AT'.

I'm a woman.
Я женщина.
Ja ZHEH-nsch'i-na.

Good, I'm going to see it.
Хорошо, я обязательно посмотрю.
Ha-ra-SHO, ja a-b'a-ZA-t'ehl'-nə pas-ma-TR'u.

So do I.
Я тоже.
Ja TO-zheh.

I'll think about it and call you tomorrow with an answer.
Я обдумаю это, и завтра позвоню вам с ответом.
Ja ab-DU-ma-ju EH-tə i ZAF-tra paz-va-N'U vam s at-V'EH-təm.

I have two children.
У меня двое детей.
U m'eh-N'A DVO-jeh d'eh-T'EHJ.

Does this place have a patio?
Здесь есть патио?
Zd'ehs' jehst' PA-t'i-o?

No, the bathroom is vacant.
Нет, уборная свободна.
N'eht, u-BOR-na-ja sva-BOD-na.

I'm not old enough.
Я не подхожу по возрасту.
Ja n'eh pad-ha-ZHU pa VOZ-rəs-tu.

No, it is very easy.
Нет, это очень просто.
N'eht, EH-tə O-ch'ehn' PROS-tə.

Understood.
Ясно.
JAS-nə.

Only if you go first.
Только если ты пойдешь первым/первой.
TOL'-kə JEH-sl'I ty paj-D'OSH P'EHR-vym/P'EHR-vəj.

Yes, that is correct.
Да, верно.
Da, V'EHR-nə.

That was the wrong answer.
Это был неправильный ответ.
Eh-tə byl n'eh-PRA-v'il'-nyj at-V'EHT.

We haven't decided yet.
Мы ещё не решили.
My jeh-SCH'o n'eh r'eh-SHY-l'i.

We can try.
Мы можем попробовать.
My MO-zhehm pap-RO-bə-vat'.

I like to read books.
Я люблю читать книги.
Ja l'ub-L'U chi-TAT' KN'I-g'i.

We can go there together.
Мы можем пойти туда вместе.
My MO-zhehm paj-T'I tu-DA VM'EH-st'eh.

Yes, I see.
Да, понятно.
Da, pa-N'AT-nə.

That looks interesting.
Выглядит интересно.
VY-gl'a-d'it in-t'eh-R'EHS-nə.

Me neither.
Я тоже.
Ja TO-zheh.

It was fun.
Было весело.
BY-lə V'EH-s'eh-lə.

Me too.
Мне тоже.
Mn'eh TO-zheh.

Stay there.
Побудьте здесь.
Pa-BUT'-t'eh zd'ehs'.

We were worried about you.
Мы волновались за тебя.
My val-na-VA-l'is' za t'eh-B'A.

No, not really.
Нет, не совсем.
N'eht, n'eh saf-S'EHM.

Unbelievable.
Невероятно.
N'eh-v'eh-ra-JAT-nə.

No, I didn't make it in time.
Нет, я не успел/успела.
N'eht ja n'eh us-P'EHL/us-P'EH-la.

No, you cannot.
Нет, нельзя.
N'eht, n'ehl'-Z'A.

Here you go.
Вот, пожалуйста.
Vot, pa-ZHA-ləs-tə.

It was good.
Было хорошо.
BY-lə ha-ra-SHO.

Ask my wife.
Спросите мою жену.
Spra-S'I-t'eh ma-JU ZHEH-nu.

That's up to him.
Это ему решать.
EH-tə jeh-MU r'eh-SHAT'.

That is not allowed.
Это запрещено.
EH-tə zap-r'eh-sch'eh-NO.

You can stay at my place.
Ты можешь остаться у меня.
Ty MO-zhehsh as-TA-tsa u m'eh-N'A.

Only if you want to.
Только если ты так хочешь.
TOL'-kə JEH-sl'I ty tak HO-chehsh.

It depends on my schedule.
Это зависит от моего графика.
EH-tə za-V'I-s'it at ma-jeh-VO GRA-f'i-ka.

I don't think that's possible.
Не думаю, что это возможно.
N'eh DU-ma-ju, shto EH-tə vaz-MOZH-nə.

You're not bothering me.
Вы мне не мешаете.
Vy mn'eh n'eh m'eh-SHA-j'eh-t'eh.

The salesman will know.
Продавец будет знать.
Pra-da-V'EHTS BU-d'eht znat'.

I have to work.
Мне надо работать.
Mn'eh NA-də ra-BO-tat'.

I'm late.
Я опаздываю.
Ja a-PAZ-dy-va-ju.

To pray.
Помолиться.
Pa-ma-L'I-tsa.

I'll do my best.
Я сделаю всё, что в моих силах.
Ja ZD'EH-la-ju fs'o, shto v ma-IH S'I-lah.

DIRECTIONS

Over here.
Здесь.
Zdes'.

Go straight ahead.
Идите прямо.
I-D'I-t'eh PR'A-mə.

Follow the straight line.
Идите по прямой.
I-D'I-t'eh pa pr'a-MOJ.

Go halfway around the circle.
Пройдите полпути по кругу.
Praj-D'I-t'eh pol-pu-T'I pa KRU-gu.

It is to the left.
Это слева.
EH-tə SL'EH-va.

Where is the party going to be?
Где будет вечеринка?
Gd'eh BU-d'eht v'eh-ch'eh-R'IN-ka?

Where is the library situated?
Где находится библиотека?
Gd'eh na-HO-d'i-tsa b'ib-l'i-a-T'EH-ka?

It is to the north.
Это на севере.
EH-tə na S'EH-v'eh-r'eh.

You can find it down the street.
Вы найдёте это ниже по улице.
Vy naj-D'O-t'eh EH-tə N'I-zheh pa U-l'i-tseh.

Go into the city to get there.
Вам нужно в город, чтобы попасть туда.
Vam NUZH-nə v GO-rəd, SHTO-by pa-PAST' tu-DA.

Where are you now?
Где вы сейчас?
Gd'eh vy s'eh-CHAS?

There is a fire hydrant right in front of me.
Прямо передо мной пожарный гидрант.
PR'A-mə P'EH-r'eh-da mnoj pa-ZHAR-nyj g'id-RANT.

Do you know a shortcut?
Вы знаете короткую дорогу?
Vy ZNA-j'eh-t'eh ka-ROT-ku-ju da-RO-gu?

Where is the freeway?
Где находится скоростная магистраль?
Gd'eh na-HO-d'i-tsa ska-ras-NA-ja ma-g'is-TRAL'?

Do I need exact change for the toll?
За проезд нужно платить без сдачи?
Za pra-JEHST NUZH-nə pla-T'IT' b'ehz ZDA-ch'i?

At the traffic light, turn right.
На светофоре поверните направо.
Na sv'eh-ta-FO-r'eh pa-v'ehr-N'I-t'eh nap-RA-və.

When you get to the intersection, turn left.
На перекрёстке поверните налево.
Na p'eh-r'eh-KR'OS-tk'eh pa-v'ehr-N'I-t'eh na-L'EH-və.

Stay in your lane until it splits off to the right.
Оставайтесь на своей полосе до первого поворота направо.
As-ta-VAJ-t'ehs' na sva-JEHJ pa-la-S'EH da P'EHR-və-va pa-va-RO-ta na-PRA-və.

Don't go onto the ramp.
Не заезжайте на пандус.
N'eh za-jeh-ZHAJ-t'eh na PAN-dus.

You are going in the wrong direction.
Вы движетесь не в ту сторону.
Vy DV'I-zheh-t'ehs' n'eh f tu STO-rə-nu.

127

Can you guide me to this location?

Вы не могли бы провести меня до этого места?

Vy n'eh mag-L'I by pra-v'ehs-T'I m'eh-N'A da EH-tə-və M'EH-sta?

Stop at the crossroads.

Остановитесь на перекрёстке.

As-ta-na-V'I-t'ehs' na p'eh-r'eh-KR'OS-tk'eh.

You missed our turn. Please turn around.

Вы пропустили наш поворот. Пожалуйста, развернитесь.

Vy pra-pus-T'I-l'i nash pa-va-ROT. Pa-ZHA-ləs-tə, raz-v'ehr-N'I-t'ehs'.

It is illegal to turn here.

Поворот сюда запрещён.

Pa-va-ROT s'u-DA zap-r'eh-SCH'ON.

We're lost, could you help us?

Мы заблудились, не могли бы вы нам помочь?

My zab-lu-D'I-l'is', n'eh mag-L'I by vy nam pa-MOCH'?

APOLOGIES

Dad, I'm sorry.
Извини, пап.
Iz-vi-N'I, pap.

I apologize for being late.
Прошу прощения за опоздание.
Pra-SHU pra-SCH'EH-n'i-ja za a-paz-DA-n'i-jeh.

Excuse me for not bringing money.
Простите, что не принёс/принесла деньги.
Pra-ST'I-t'eh, shto n'eh pr'i-N'OS/pr'i-n'ehs-LA D'EHN'-g'i.

That was my fault.
Это моя вина.
EH-tə ma-JA v'i-NA.

It won't happen again, I'm sorry.
Этого больше не повторится, извините.
EH-tə-və BOL'-sheh n'eh paf-ta-R'I-tsa, iz-v'i-N'I-t'eh.

I won't break another promise.
Я больше не нарушу своё обещание.
Ja BOL'-sheh n'eh na-RU-shu sva-JO a-b'eh-SCHA-n'i-jeh.

You have my word that I'll be careful.
Даю слово, я буду осторожен/осторожна.
Da-JU SLO-və, ja BU-du as-ta-RO-zhehn/as-ta-ROZH-na.

I'm sorry, I wasn't paying attention.
Простите, я был/была невнимателен/невнимательна.
Pra-ST'I-t'eh, ja byl/by-LA n'eh-vn'i-MA-t'eh-l'ehn/n'eh-vn'i-MA-t'ehl'-na.

I regret that. I'm so sorry.
Я сожалею об этом. Мне так жаль.
Ja sa-zha-L'EH-ju ab EH-təm. Mn'eh tak zhal'.

I'm sorry, but today I can't.

Прости, но сегодня я не могу.

Pras-T'I, no s'eh-VO-dn'a ja n'eh ma-GU.

It's not your fault, I'm sorry.

Это не твоя вина, мне жаль.

EH-tə n'eh tva-JA v'i-NA, mn'eh zhal'.

Please, give me another chance.

Пожалуйста, дай мне ещё один шанс.

Pa-ZHA-ləs-tə, daj mn'eh jeh-SCH'O a-D'IN shans.

Will you ever forgive me?

Ты когда-нибудь простишь меня?

Ty kag-DA-n'i-but' pras-T'ISH m'eh-N'A?

I hope in time we can still be friends.

Надеюсь, когда-нибудь мы снова сможем быть друзьями.

Na-D'EH-jus', kag-DA-n'i-but' my SNO-və SMO-zhehm byt' druz'-JA-m'i.

I screwed up, and I'm sorry.

Я напортачил/напортачила, и мне жаль.

Ja na-par-TA-chil/na-par-TA-chi-la i mn'eh zhal'.

SMALL TALK

No.
Нет.
N'eht.

Yes.
Да.
Da.

Okay.
Хорошо.
Ha-ra-SHO.

Please.
Пожалуйста.
Pa-ZHA-ləs-tə.

Do you fly out of the country often?
Вы часто летаете за границу?
Vy CHAS-tə l'eh-TA-j'eh-t'eh za gra-N'I-tsu?

Thank you.
Спасибо.
Spa-S'I-bə.

That's okay.
Ничего страшного.
N'i-ch'eh-VO STRASH-nə-və.

I went shopping.
Я пошёл/пошла за покупками.
Ja pa-SHOL/pash-LA za pa-KUP-ka-m'i.

There.
Вот.
Vot.

Very well.
Очень хорошо.
O'chehn' ha-ra-SHO.

What?
Что?
Shto?

I think you'll like it.
Думаю, вам это понравится.
DU-ma-ju, vam EH-tə pan-RA-v'i-tsa.

When?
Когда?
Kag-DA?

I didn't sleep well.
Я плохо спал/спала.
Ja PLO-hə SPAL/spa-LA.

Until what time?
До какого часа?
Do ka-KO-və CHA-sa?

We are waiting in line.
Мы стоим в очереди.
My sta-IM v O-ch'eh-r'eh-d'i.

We're only waiting for a little bit longer.
Мы подождём ещё совсем немного.
My pa-dazh-D'OM jeh-SCH'O saf-S'EHM n'eh-MNO-gə.

How?
Как?
Kak?

Where?
Где?
Gd'eh?

I'm glad.
Я рад/рада.
Ja rat/RA-da.

You are very tall.
Вы очень высокий/высокая.
Vy O-chen' vy-SO-k'ij/vy-SO-ka-ja.

I like to speak your language.
Мне нравится говорить на вашем языке.
Mn'eh NRA-v'i-tsa ga-va-R'IT' na VA-shehm jə-zy-K'EH.

You are very kind.
Вы очень добры.
Vy O-chen' dab-RY.

Happy birthday!
С Днём рождения!
S dn'om razh-D'EH-n'i-ja.

I would like to thank you very much.
Я очень вам благодарен/благодарна.
Ja O-ch'ehn' vam bla-ga-DA-r'ehn/bla-ga-DAR-na.

Here is a gift that I bought for you.
Вот подарок, который я тебе купил/купила.
Vot pa-DA-rək, ka-TO-ryj ja t'eh-B'EH ku-P'IL/ku-P'I-la.

Yes. Thank you for all of your help.
Да. Спасибо за вашу помощь.
Da. Spa-S'I-bə za VA-shu PO-məsch.

What did you get?
Что ты принёс/принесла?
Shto ty pr'i-N'OS/pr'i-n'ehs-LA?

Have a good trip!
Счастливого пути!
Sch'as-L'I-və-və pu-T'I!

This place is very special to me.
Это место мне очень дорого.
EH-tə M'EHS-tə mn'eh O-ch'ehn' DO-rə-gə.

My foot is asleep.
У меня онемела нога.
U m'eh-N'A a-n'eh-M'EH-la na-GA.

May I open this now or later?

Мне открыть это сейчас или позже?

Mn'eh at-KRYT' EH-tə s'eh-CHAS I-l'i POZ-zheh?

Why do you think that is?

Как ты думаешь, почему это так?

Kak ty DU-ma-jehsh, pa-cheh-MU EH-tə tak?

Which do you like better, chocolate or caramel?

Что тебе нравится больше, шоколад или карамель?

Shto t'eh-B'EH NRA-v'i-tsa BOL'sheh, sha-ka-LAD I-l'i ka-ra-M'EHL'?

Be safe on your journey.

Будь осторожен/осторожна в пути.

But' asta-RO-zhehn/as-ta-ROZH-na f pu-T'I.

I want to do this for a little longer.

Я хочу позаниматься этим ещё немного.

Ja ha-CHU pa-za-n'i-MA-tsa EH-t'im jeh-SCH'O n'eh-MNO-gə.

This is a picture that I took at the hotel.

Вот фотография, которую я сделал/сделала в отеле.

Vot fa-tag-RA-f'i-ja, ka-TO-ru-ju ja ZD'EH-lal/ZD'EH-la-la v a-TEH-l'eh.

Allow me.

Позвольте мне.

Paz-VOL'-t'eh mn'eh.

I was surprised.

Я был удивлен/была удивлена.

Ja byl u-d'iv-L'ON/by-LA u-d'iv-l'eh-NA.

I like that.

Мне это нравится.

Mn'eh EH-tə NRA-v'i-tsa.

Are you in high spirits today?

Ты сегодня в хорошем настроении?

Ty s'eh-VO-dn'a f ha-RO-sh'ehm nas-tra-JEH-n'i-i?

Oh, here comes my wife.

А вот и моя жена.

A vot i ma-JA zheh-NA.

Can I see the photograph?
Можно посмотреть фото?
MOZH-nə pas-mat-R'EHT' FO-tə?

Feel free to ask me anything.
Не стесняйтесь, спрашивайте меня о чём угодно.
N'eh st'ehs-N'AJ-t'ehs', SPRA-shy-vaj-t'eh m'eh-N'A a ch'om u-GOD-nə.

That was magnificent!
Это было великолепно!
EH-tə BY-lə ve-l'i-ka-L'EH-pnə.

See you some other time.
Увидимся позже.
U-V'I-d'im-s'a PO-zheh.

No more, please.
Спасибо, достаточно.
Spa-S'I-bə, das-TA-təch-nə.

Please don't use that.
Пожалуйста, не используйте это.
Pa-ZHA-ləs-tə, n'eh is-POL'-zuj-t'eh EH-tə.

That is very pretty.
Это очень красиво.
EH-tə O-ch'ehn' kra-S'I-və.

Would you say that again?
Повторите, пожалуйста.
Paf-ta-R'I-t'eh, pa-ZHA-ləs-ta.

Speak slowly.
Говорите медленно.
Ga-va-R'I-t'eh M'EHD-l'eh-nə.

I'm home.
Я дома.
Ja DO-ma.

Is this your home?
Это твой дом?
EH-tə tvoj dom?

I know a lot about the area.
Я много знаю об этом районе.
Ja MNO-gə ZNA-ju ab EH-təm ra-JO-n'eh.

Welcome back. How was your day?
Добро пожаловать домой. Как прошёл твой день?
Da-BRO pa-ZHA-lə-vat' da-MOJ. Kak pra-SHOL tvoj d'ehn'?

I read every day.
Я читаю каждый день.
Ja chi-TA-ju KAZH-dyj d'ehn'.

My favorite type of book is novels by Stephen King.
Мои любимые книги — это романы Стивена Кинга.
Ma-I l'u-B'I-my-jeh KN'I-g'i — EH-tə ra-MA-ny ST'I-v'eh-na K'IN-ga.

You surprised me!
Ты меня удивил/удивила!
Ty m'eh-N'A u-d'i-V'IL/u-d'i-V'I-la.

I am short on time so I have to go.
У меня мало времени, так что мне нужно идти.
U m'eh-N'A MA-lə VR'EH-m'eh-n'i, tak shto mn'eh NU-zhnə i-T'I.

Thank you for having this conversation.
Спасибо за разговор.
Spa-S'I-bə za raz-ga-VOR.

Oh, when is it?
О, когда?
O, kag-DA?

This is my brother, Jeremy.
Это мой брат, Джереми.
EH-tə moj brat DZHEH-r'eh-m'i.

That is my favorite bookstore.
Это мой любимый книжный магазин.
EH-tə moj l'u-B'I-myj KNIZH-nyj ma-ga-Z'IN.

That statue is bigger than it looks.
Эта статуя больше, чем кажется.
EH-tə STA-tu-ja BOL'-sheh, ch'ehm KA-zheh-tsa.

Look at the shape of that cloud!

Посмотри на форму этого облака!

Pas-mat-R'I na FOR-mu EH-tə-və OB-la-ka!

BUSINESS

I am president of the credit union.

Я председатель кредитного союза.

Ja pr'eh-ds'eh-DA-t'ehl' kr'eh-D'IT-nə-və sa-JU-za.

We are expanding in your area.

Мы расширяемся в вашем районе.

My ras-shy-R'A-jehm-s'a v VA-shehm ra-JO-n'eh.

I am looking for work in the agriculture field.

Я ищу работу в области сельского хозяйства.

Ja i-SCH'U ra-BO-tu v OB-las-t'i S'EHL'-skə-və ha-Z'AJ-stvə.

Sign here, please.

Распишитесь здесь, пожалуйста.

Ras-p'i-SHY-t'ehs' zd'ehs', pa-ZHA-ləs-tə.

I am looking for temporary work.

Я ищу временную работу.

Ja i-SCH'U VR'EH-m'ehn-nu-ju ra-BO-tu.

I need to call and set up that meeting.

Мне нужно позвонить и организовать эту встречу.

Mn'eh NUZH-nə paz-va-n'iT' i ar-ga-n'i-za-VAT' EH-tu FSTR'EH-chu.

Is the line open?

Линия открыта?

L'I-n'i-ja at-KRY-ta?

I need you to hang up the phone.

Мне нужно, чтобы вы повесили трубку.

Mn'eh NUZH-nə, SHTO-by vy pa-V'EH-s'i-l'i TRUP-ku.

Who should I ask for more information about your business?

У кого я могу узнать больше о вашей компании?

U ka-VO ja ma-GU uz-NAT' BOL'-sheh a VA-shehj kam-PA-n'i-i?

There was no answer when you handed me the phone.
Когда вы передали мне телефон, в трубке была тишина.
Kag-DA vy p'eh-r'eh-DA-l'i mn'eh t'eh-l'eh-FON, f TRUP-k'eh by-LA t'i-sh'i-NA.

Robert is not here at the moment.
Роберта сейчас нет.
RO-b'ehr-ta s'eh-CHAS n'eht.

Call me after work, thanks.
Позвоните мне после работы, спасибо.
Paz-va-N'I-t'eh mn'eh POS-l'eh ra-BO-ty, spa-S'I-bə.

We're strongly considering your contract offer.
Мы серьёзно рассматриваем ваше предложение о контракте.
My s'eh-R'JOZ-nə ras-SMAT-r'i-va-jehm VA-sheh pr'ehd-la-ZHEH-n'i-jeh a kan-TRAK-t'eh.

Have the necessary forms been signed yet?
Вы уже подписали необходимые документы?
Vy u-ZHEH pat-p'i-SA-l'i n'eh-ab-ha-D'I-my-jeh da-ku-M'EHN-ty?

I have a few hours available after work.
У меня есть несколько свободных часов после работы.
U m'eh-N'A jehst' N'EHS-kəl-kə sva-BOD-nyh cha-SOF POS-l'eh ra-BO-ty.

What do they make there?
Что здесь производят?
Shto zd'ehs' pra-iz-VO-d'at?

I have no tasks assigned to me.
Мне не дали никаких заданий.
Mn'eh n'eh DA-l'i ni-ka-K'IH za-DA-n'ij.

How many workers are they hiring?
Сколько работников они нанимают?
SKOL'-kə ra-BOT-n'i-kəf a-N'I na-n'i-MA-jut?

It should take me three hours to complete this task.
Мне понадобится три часа, чтобы выполнить это задание.
Mn'eh pa-NA-də-b'i-tsa tr'i cha-SA, SHTO-by VY-pal-n'it' EH-tə za-DA-n'i-jeh.

Don't use that computer, it is only for financial work.
Не используйте этот компьютер, он только для финансовой работы.
N'eh is-POL'-zuj-t'eh EH-təT kam-PJU-tər, on TOL'-kə dl'a f'i-NAN-sə-vəj ra-BO-ty.

I only employ people that I can rely on.
Я нанимаю только тех, на кого могу положиться.
Ja na-n'i-MA-ju TOL'-kə t'ehh, na ka-VO ma-GU pa-la-ZHY-tsa.

After I talk to my lawyers, we can discuss this further.
Мы можем обсудить это дальше, когда я поговорю со своими адвокатами.
My MO-zhehm ap-su-D'IT' EH-tə DAL'-sheh, kag-DA ja pa-ga-va-R'U sa sva-I-m'i ad-va-KA-tə-m'i.

Are there any open positions in my field?
Есть ли свободные должности по моей специальности?
Jehst' l'i sva-BOD-ny-jeh DOL-zhnas-t'i pa ma-JEHJ sp'eh-tsy-AL'-nəs-t'i?

I'll meet you in the conference room.
Встретимся в конференц-зале.
FSTR'EH-t'im-s'a f kan-f'eh-R'EHNTS ZA-l'eh.

Call and leave a message on my office phone.
Позвоните на мой рабочий телефон и оставьте сообщение.
Paz-va-N'I-t'eh na moj ra-BO-chij t'eh-l'eh-FON i as-TAF'-t'eh sa-ap-SCH'EH-n'i-jeh.

Send me a fax with that information.
Пришлите мне факс с этой информацией.
Pr'ish-L'I-t'eh mn'eh faks s EH-təj in-far-MA-tsy-jehj.

Hi, I would like to leave a message for Sheila.
Здравствуйте, я бы хотел/хотела оставить сообщение для Шейлы.
ZDRA-stvuj-t'eh, ja by ha-T'EHL/ha-T'EH-la as-TA-v'it' sa-ap-SCH'EH-n'i-jeh dl'a SHEHJ-ly.

Please repeat your last name.
Пожалуйста, повторите вашу фамилию.
Pa-ZHA-ləs-tə, paf-ta-R'I-t'eh VA-shu fa-M'I-l'i-ju.

I would like to buy wholesale.
Я бы хотел/хотела купить оптом.
Ja by ha-T'EHL/ha-T'EH-la ku-P'IT' OP-təm.

How do you spell your last name?

Как пишется ваша фамилия?

Kak P'I-sheh-tsa VA-sha fa-M'I-l'i-ja?

I called your boss yesterday and left a message.

Я вчера звонил/звонила вашему начальнику и оставил/оставила сообщение.

Ja vch'eh-RA zva-N'IL/zva-N'I-la VA-sheh-mu na-CHAL'-n'i-ku i as-TA-v'il/as-TA-v'i-la sa-ap-SCH'EH'-n'i-jeh.

That customer hung up on me.

Клиент повесил трубку.

Kl'i-JEHNT pa-V'EH-s'il TRUP-ku.

She called but didn't leave a callback number.

Она звонила, но не оставила номер, по которому можно перезвонить.

A-NA zva-N'I-la, no n'eh as-TA-v'i-la NO-m'ehr, pa ka-TO-rəmu MOZH-nə p'eh-r'eh-zva-N'IT'.

Hello! Am I speaking to Bob?

Алло! Это Боб?

A-LO! EH-tə bob?

Excuse me, but could you speak up? I can't hear you.

Извините, вы не могли бы говорить громче? Я вас не слышу.

Iz-v'i-N'I-t'eh, vy n'eh mag-L'I by ga-va-R'IT' GROM-ch'eh? Ja vas n'eh SLY-shu.

The line is very bad, could you move to a different area so I can hear you better?

Сеть очень плохая, вы не могли бы перейти куда-нибудь, чтобы я мог/могла вас лучше слышать?

S'eht' O-ch'ehn' pla-HA-ja, vy n'eh mag-L'I by p'eh-r'ehj-T'I ku-DA-n'i-but', SHTO-by ja mog/mag-LA vas LU-chsheh SLY-shat'?

I would like to apply for a work visa.

Я бы хотел/хотела подать заявление на получение рабочей визы.

Ja by ha-T'EHL/ha-T'EH-la pa-DAT' za-jav-L'EH-n'i-jeh na pa-lu-CH'EH-n'i-jeh ra-BO-chehj V'I-zy.

141

It is my dream to work here teaching the language.
Моя мечта работать здесь и преподавать язык.
Ma-JA m'ehch-TA ra-BO-tat' zd'ehs' i pr'eh-pa-da-VAT' jə-ZYK.

I have always wanted to work here.
Я всегда хотел/хотела работать здесь.
Ja fs'ehg-DA ha-T'EHL/ha-T'EH-la ra-BO-tat' zd'ehs'.

Where do you work?
Где вы работаете?
Gd'eh vy ra-BO-ta-j'eh-t'eh?

Are we in the same field of work?
Мы работаем в одной области?
My ra-BO-ta-jehm v ad-NOJ OB-las-t'i?

Do we share an office?
Мы работаем в одном офисе?
My ra-BO-ta-jehm v ad-NOM O-f'i-s'eh?

What do you do for a living?
Кем вы работаете?
K'ehm vy ra-BO-ta-j'eh-t'eh?

I work in the city as an engineer for Cosco.
Я работаю в городе инженером в Cosco.
Ja ra-BO-ta-ju v GO-rə-de in-zheh-N'EH-rəm f Cosco.

I am an elementary teacher.
Я учитель/учительница начальных классов.
Ja u-CHI-t'ehl'/ u-CHI-t'ehl'-n'i-tsa na-CHAL'-nyh KLA-səf.

What time should I be at the meeting?
Во сколько я должен/должна быть на собрании?
Va SKOL'-kə ja DOL-zhehn/dal-ZHNA byt' na sab-RA-n'i-i?

Would you like me to catch you up on what the meeting was about?
Мне рассказать вам, о чём говорилось на собрании?
Mn'eh ras-ka-ZAT' vam, a ch'om ga-va-R'I-ləs' na sab-RA-n'i-i?

I would like to set up a meeting with your company.
Я бы хотел/хотела организовать встречу с вашей компанией.
Ja by ha-T'EHL/ha-T'EH-la ar-ga-n'i-za-VAT' FSTR'EH-chu s VA-shehj kam-PA-n'i-jehj.

Please, call my secretary for that information.
Пожалуйста, позвоните моему секретарю, чтобы узнать эту информацию.
Pa-ZHA-ləs-tə, paz-va-N'I-t'eh ma-jeh-MU s'ehk-r'eh-ta-R'U, SHTO-by uz-NAT' EH-tu in-far-MA-tsy-ju.

I will have to ask my lawyer.
Мне придётся спросить моего адвоката.
Mn'eh pr'i-D'O-tsa spra-S'IT' ma-jeh-VO ad-va-KA-ta.

Fax it over to my office number.
Отправьте это по факсу на номер моего офиса.
At-PRAF'-t'eh EH-tə pa FA-ksu na NO-m'ehr ma-jeh-VO O-f'i-sa.

Will I have any trouble calling into the office?
У меня могут быть проблемы с тем, чтобы позвонить в офис?
U m'eh-N'A MO-gut byt' prab-L'EH-my s t'ehm SHTO-by paz-va-N'IT v O-f'is?

Do you have a business card I can have?
У вас есть визитная карточка, которую вы могли бы мне дать?
U vas jehst' v'i-Z'IT-na-ja KAR-təch-ka, ka-TO-ru-ju vy mag-L'I by mn'eh dat'?

Here is my business card. Please, take it.
Вот моя визитная карточка. Пожалуйста, возьмите.
Vot ma-JA v'i-Z'IT-na-ja KAR-təch-ka. Pa-ZHA-ləs-tə, vaz'-M'I-t'eh.

My colleague and I are going to lunch.
Мы с коллегой собираемся на обед.
My s ka-L'EH-gəj sa-b'i-RA-jehm-s'a na a'B'EHD.

I am the director of finance for my company.
Я финансовый директор своей компании.
Ja f'i-NAN-sə-vyj d'i-R'EHK-tər sva-JEHJ kam-PA-n'i-i.

I manage the import goods of my company.
Я занимаюсь импортом товаров для своей компании.
Ja za-n'i-MA-jus' IM-pər-təm ta-VA-rəf dl'a sva-JEHJ kam-PA-n'i-i.

My colleagues' boss is Steven.
Начальника моих коллег зовут Стивен.
Na-CHAL'-n'i-ka ma-IH ka-L'EHG za-VUT ST'I-v'ehn.

I work for the gas station company.

Я работаю на команию автозаправок.

Ja ra-BO-ta-ju na kam-PA-n'i-ju afta-zap-RA-vək.

What company do you work for?

На какую компанию вы работаете?

Na ka-KU-ju kam-PA-n'i-ju vy ra-BO-ta-j'eh-t'eh?

I'm an independent contractor.

Я независимый подрядчик.

Ja n'eh-za-V'I-s'i-myj pad-R'AT-chik.

How many employees do you have at your company?

Сколько сотрудников в вашей компании?

SKOL'-kə sat-RUD-n'i-kəf v VA-shehj kam-PA-n'i-i?

I know a lot about engineering.

Я хорошо разбираюсь в инженерии.

Ja ha-ra-SHO raz-b'i-RA-jus' v in-zheh-N'EH-r'i-i.

I can definitely resolve that dispute for you.

Я, конечно же, могу разрешить этот конфликт для вас.

Ja ka-N'EH-shnə zheh ma-GU raz-r'eh-SHYT' EH-tət kan-FL'IKT dl'a vas.

You should hire an interpreter.

Вам следует нанять переводчика.

Vam SL'EH-du-jeht na-N'AT' p'eh-r'eh-VOT-chi-ka.

Are you hiring any additional workers?

Вы нанимаете дополнительных работников?

Vy na-n'i-MA-j'eh-t'eh da-pal-N'I-t'ehl'-nyh ra-BOT-n'i-kəf?

How much experience do I need to work here?

Сколько опыта мне нужно, чтобы работать здесь?

SKOL'-kə O-py-ta mn'eh NUZH-nə, SHTO-by ra-BO-tat' zd'ehs'?

Our marketing manager handles that.

Наш менеджер по маркетингу занимается этим.

Nash MEH-neh-dzher pa mar-K'EH-t'in-gu za-n'i-MA-jeh-tsa EH-t'im.

I would like to poach one of your workers.

Я бы хотел/хотела «украсть» одного из ваших работников.

Ja by ha-T'EHL/ha-T'EH-la uk-RAST' ad-na-VO iz VA-shyh ra-BOT-n'i-kəf.

Can we work out a deal that is beneficial for the both of us?

Мы можем придумать сделку, которая будет выгодна нам обоим?

My MO-zhehm pr'i-DU-mat' ZD'EHL-ku, ka-TO-ra-ja BU-d'eht VY-gə-dna nam a-BO-im?

My resources are at your disposal.

Мои ресурсы в вашем распоряжении.

Ma-I r'eh-SUR-sy v VA-shehm ras-pa-r'a-ZHEH-n'i-i.

I am afraid that we have to let you go.

Боюсь, нам придётся вас уволить.

Ba-JUS' nam pr'i-D'O-tsa vas u-VO-l'it'.

This is your first warning. Please don't do that again.

Это ваше первое предупреждение. Пожалуйста, не делайте этого больше.

EH-tə VA-sheh P'EHR-va-jeh pr'eh-dup-r'ehzh-D'EH-n'i-jeh. Pa-ZHA-ləs-tə, n'eh DE-laj-t'eh EH-tə-və BOL'-sheh.

File a complaint with HR about the incident.

Подайте жалобу об этом случае менеджеру отдела кадров.

Pa-DAJ-t'eh ZHA-lə-bu ab EH-təm SLU-cha-jeh MEH-neh-dzheh-ru at-D'EH-la KAD-rəf.

Who is showing up for our lunch meeting?

Кто будет на нашем деловом ланче?

Kto BU-d'eht na NA-shehm d'eh-la-VOM LAN-ch'eh?

Clear out the rest of my day.

Освободите остаток моего дня.

As-va-ba-D'I-t'eh as-TA-tək ma-jeh-VO dn'a.

We need to deposit this into the bank.

Нам нужно положить это в банк.

Nam NUZH-nə pa-la-ZHYT' EH-tə v bank.

Can you cover the next hour for me?

Ты не мог/могла бы подменить меня на следующий час?

Ty n'eh mog/mag-LA by pad-m'eh-N'IT' m'eh-N'A na SL'EH-du-schij chas?

If Shania calls, please push her directly through.

Если позвонит Шания, пожалуйста, соедините нас напрямую.

JEH-sl'i paz-va-N'IT SHA-n'i-ja, pa-ZHA-ləs-tə, sa-jeh-d'i-N'I-t'eh nas na-pr'a-MU-ju.

I'm leaving early today.
Сегодня я ухожу раньше.
S'eh-VO-dn'a ja u-ha-ZHU RAN'-sheh.

I'll be working late tonight.
Сегодня я буду работать допоздна.
S'eh-VO-dn'a ja BU-du ra-BO-tat' da-paz-NA.

You can use the bathroom in my office.
Вы можете воспользоваться уборной в моем офисе.
Vy MO-zheh-t'eh vas-POL'-zə-va-tsa u-BOR-nəj v ma-JOM O-f'i-seh.

You can use my office phone to call out.
Вы можете воспользоваться телефоном в моём кабинете, чтобы позвонить.
Vy MO-zheh-t'eh vas-POL'-zə-va-tsa t'eh-l'eh-FO-nəm v ma-JOM ka-bi-N'EH-t'eh, SHTO-by paz-va-N'IT'.

Please, close the door behind you.
Пожалуйста, закройте за собой дверь.
Pa-ZHA-ləs-tə, zak-ROJ-t'eh za sa-BOJ dv'ehr'.

I need to talk to you privately.
Мне нужно поговорить с вами наедине.
Mn'eh NUZH-nə pa-ga-va-R'IT' s VA-m'i na-jeh-d'i-N'EH.

Your team is doing good work on this project.
Ваша команда хорошо справляется с этим проектом.
VA-sha ka-MAN-da ha-ra-SHO spra-VL'A-jeh-tsa s EH-t'im pra-EHK-təm.

Our numbers are down this quarter.
В этом квартале наши показатели снизились.
V EH-təm kvar-TA-l'eh NA-shy pa-ka-ZA-t'eh-l'i SN'I-z'i-l'is'.

I need you to work harder than usual.
Мне нужно, чтобы вы работали усерднее, чем обычно.
Mn'eh NUZH-nə, SHTO-by vy ra-BO-ta-l'i u-S'ER-dn'eh-jeh, ch'ehm a-BYCH-nə.

I'm calling in sick today. Can anyone cover my shift?
Я сегодня на больничном. Кто-нибудь может меня подменить?
Ja s'eh-VO-dn'a na bal'-N'ICH-nəm. KTO-n'i-but' MO-zheht m'eh-N'A pad-m'eh-N'IT'?

Tom, we are thinking of promoting you.

Том, мы думаем повысить тебя.

Tom, my DU-ma-jehm pa-VY-s'it' t'eh-B'A.

I would like a raise.

Я бы хотел/хотела получить прибавку к зарплате.

Ja by ha-T'EHL/ha-T'EH-la pa-lu-CHIT' pr'i-BAF-ku k zar-PLA-t'eh.

THE WEATHER

I think the weather is changing.
Думаю, погода изменится.
DU-ma-ju, pa-GO-da iz-M'EH-n'i-tsa.

Be careful, it is raining outside.
Будь осторожен/осторожна, на улице идёт дождь.
But' as-ta-RO-zhehn/as-ta-ROZH-na, na U-l'i-tseh i-D'OT dosht'.

Make sure to bring your umbrella.
Не забудь взять зонтик.
N'eh za-BUT' vz'at' ZON-t'ik.

Get out of the rain or you will catch a cold.
Не ходи под дождём, а то простудишься.
N'eh ha-D'I pad dazh-D'OM, a to pras-TU-d'ish-s'a.

Is it snowing?
Идёт снег?
I-D'OT sn'ehk?

The snow is very thick right now.
Снег сейчас очень густой.
Sn'ehk s'eh-CHAS O-chehn' gus-TOJ.

Be careful, the road is full of ice.
Будь осторожен/осторожна, дорога вся покрыта льдом.
But' as-ta-RO-zhehn/as-ta-RO-zhna, da-RO-ga fs'a pak-RY-ta l'dom.

What is the climate like here? Is it warm or cold?
Какой здесь климат? Тёплый или холодный?
Ka-KOJ zd'ehs' KL'I-mat? T'OP-lyj I-l'i ha-LOD-nyj?

It has been a very nice temperature here.
Температура здесь была очень приятной.
T'ehm-p'eh-ra-TU-ra zd'ehs' by-LA O-ch'ehn' pr'i-JAT-nəj.

Does it rain a lot here?
Здесь часто идёт дождь?
Zd'ehs' CHAS-tə i-D'OT dosht'?

The temperature is going to break records this week.
На этой неделе будет побит температурный рекорд.
Na EH-təj n'eh-D'EH-l'eh BU-d'eht pa-B'IT t'ehm-p'eh-ra-TUR-nyj r'eh-KORT.

Does it ever snow here?
Здесь когда-нибудь идёт снег?
Zd'ehs' kag-DA-n'i-but' i-D'OT sn'ehk?

When does it get sunny?
Когда становится солнечно?
Kag-DA sta-NO-v'i-tsa SOL-n'ehch-nə?

What's the forecast look like for tomorrow?
Какой прогноз погоды на завтра?
Ka-KOJ prag-NOS pa-GO-dy na ZAF-tra?

This is a heatwave.
Это жара.
EH-tə zha-RA.

Right now, it is overcast, but it should clear up by this evening.
Сейчас пасмурно, но к вечеру должно проясниться.
S'eh-CHAS PAS-mur-nə, no k V'EH-ch'eh-ru dal-ZHNO pra-jəs-N'I-tsa.

It is going to heat up in the afternoon.
После обеда потеплеет.
POS-l'eh a-B'EH-da pa-t'ehp-L'EH-jeht.

What channel is the weather channel?
По какому каналу показывают погоду?
Pa ka-KO-mu ka-NA-lu pa-KA-zy-va-jut pa-GO-du?

Tonight it will be below freezing.
Сегодня ночью будет ниже нуля.
S'eh-VO-dn'a NO-ch'ju BU-d'eht N'I-zheh nu-L'A.

It's very windy outside.
На улице очень ветрено.
Na U-l'i-tseh O'chehn' V'EH-tr'eh-nə.

It's going to be cold in the morning.
Утром будет холодно.
U-trəm BU-d'eht HO-ləd-nə.

It's not raining, only drizzling.
Дождя нет, просто морось.
Dazh-D'A n'eht, PROS-tə MO-rəs'.

HOTEL

I would like to book a room.
Я бы хотел/хотела забронировать комнату.
Ja by ha-T'EHL/ha-T'EH-la zab-ra-N'I-rə-vət' KOM-na-tu.

I'd like a single room.
Я бы хотел/хотела одноместный номер.
Ja by ha-T'EHL/ha-T'EH-la ad-na-M'EHS-nyj NO-m'ehr.

I'd like a suite.
Я бы хотел/хотела люкс.
Ja by ha-T'EHL/ha-T'EH-la l'uks.

How much is the room per night?
Сколько стоит номер за ночь?
SKOL'-kə STO-it NO-m'ehr ZA nəch?

How much is the room with tax?
Сколько стоит номер с НДС?
SKOL'-kə STO-it NO-m'ehr s ehn-deh-EHS?

When is the checkout time?
Во сколько нужно выписаться?
Va SKOL'-kə NUZH-nə VY-p'i-sa-tsa?

I'd like a room with a nice view.
Я бы хотел/хотела номер с красивым видом.
Ja by ha-T'EHL/ha-T'EH-la NO-m'ehr s kra-S'I-vym V'I-dəm.

I'd like to order room service.
Я бы хотел/хотела попросить обслуживание номеров.
Ja by ha-T'EHL/ha-T'EH-la pap-ra-S'IT' ap-SLU-zhy-va-n'i-jeh na-m'eh-ROF.

Let's go swim in the outdoor pool.
Пойдём поплаваем в открытом бассейне.
Paj-D'OM pap-LA-va-jehm v at-KRY-təm ba-S'EHJ-n'eh.

Are pets allowed at the hotel?

В этом отеле можно останавливаться с животными?

V EH-təm a-TEH-l'eh MOZH-nə as-ta-NAV-l'i-va-tsa s zhy-VOT-ny-m'i?

I would like a room on the first floor.

Я бы хотел/хотела номер на первом этаже.

Ja by ha-T'EHL/ha-T'EH-la NO-m'ehr na P'EHR-vəm eh-ta-ZHEH.

Can you send maintenance up to our room for a repair?

Не могли бы вы отправить кого-нибудь из обслуживающего персонала в наш номер для ремонта?

N'eh mag-L'I by vy at-PRA-v'it' ka-VO-n'i-but' iz ap-SLU-zhy-va-ju-scheh-və p'ehr-sa-NA-la v nash NO-m'ehr dl'a r'eh-MON-ta?

I'm locked out of my room, could you unlock it?

У меня захлопнулась дверь, не могли бы вы открыть её?

U m'eh-N'A zah-LOP-nu-las' dv'ehr', n'eh mag-L'I by vy at-KRYT' jeh-JO?

Our door is jammed and won't open.

Мою дверь заело, и она не открывается.

Ma-JU dv'ehr' za-JEH-lə, i a-NA n'eh at-kry-VA-jeh-tsa.

How do you work the shower?

Как включить душ?

Kak fkl'u-CHIT' dush?

Are the consumables in the room free?

Еда, напитки и прочие товары в номере бесплатные?

Jeh-DA, na-P'I-tk'i i PRO-chi-jeh ta-VA-ry v NO-m'eh-r'eh b'ehs-PLAT-ny-jeh?

What is my final bill for the stay, including incidentals?

Какой мой окончательный счёт за пребывание, включая непредвиденные расходы?

Ka-KOJ moj a-kan-CHA-t'ehl'-nyj sch'ot za pr'eh-by-VA-n'i-jeh, fkl'u-CHA-ja n'eh-pr'ehd-V'I-d'eh-ny-jeh ras-HO-dy?

Can you show me to my room?

Не могли бы вы показать мне мой номер?

N'eh mag-L'I by vy pa-ka-ZAT' mn'eh moj NO-m'ehr?

Where can I get ice for my room?

Где я могу взять лёд для своего номера?

Gd'eh ja ma-GU vz'at' l'od dl'a sva-jeh-VO NO-m'eh-ra?

Do you have any rooms available?
У вас есть свободные номера?
U vas jehst' sva-BOD-ny-jeh na-m'eh-RA?

Do you sell bottled water?
Вы продаете воду в бутылках?
Vy pra-da-JO-t'eh VO-du v bu-TYL-kah?

Our towels are dirty.
Наши полотенца грязные.
NA-shy pa-la-T'EHN-tsa GR'AZ-ny-jeh.

Have you stayed at this hotel before?
Вы раньше останавливались в этом отеле?
Vy RAN'-sheh as-ta-NAV-l'i-va-l'is' v EH-təm a-TEH-l'eh?

How much is a room for two adults?
Сколько стоит номер для двоих взрослых?
SKOL'-kə STO-it NO-m'ehr dl'a dva-IH VZROS-lyh?

Does the room come with a microwave?
В номере есть микроволновая печь?
V NO-m'eh-r'eh jehst' m'ik-ra-val-NO-va-ja p'ehch?

May I see the room first? That way I will know if I like it.
Могу я сначала посмотреть номер? Так я буду знать, понравится ли он мне.
Ma-GU ja sna-CHA-la pas-mat-R'EHT' NO-m'ehr? Tak ja BU-du znat', pan-RA-v'i-tsa l'i on mn'eh.

Do you have a room that is quieter?
У вас есть менее шумная комната?
U vas jehst' M'EH-n'eh-jeh SHUM-na-ja KOM-na-ta?

How much is the deposit for my stay?
Каков задаток за моё пребывание?
Ka-KOF za-DA-tək za ma-JO pr'eh-by-VA-n'i-jeh?

Is the tap water drinkable at the hotel?
В этом отеле можно пить воду из-под крана?
V EH-təm a-TEH-l'e MOZH-nə p'it' VO-du IS-pət KRA-na?

Will there be any holds on my credit card?
Вы удержите средства с моей кредитной карты?
Vy u-D'EHR-zhy-t'eh SR'EHD-stva s ma-JEHJ kr'eh-D'IT-nəj KAR-ty?

Can I get a replacement room key?
Можно мне запасной ключ от номера?
MOZH-nə mn'eh za-pas-NOJ kl'uch' at NO-m'eh-ra?

How much is a replacement room key?
Сколько стоит запасной ключ от номера?
SKOL'-kə STO-it za-pas-NOJ kl'uch at NO-m'eh-ra?

Does the bathroom have a shower or a bathtub?
В ванной комнате душ или ванна?
V VAN-nəj KOM-na-t'eh dush I-l'i VA-nna?

Are any of the channels on the TV available in English?
Есть ли телевизионные каналы на английском языке?
Jehst' l'i t'eh-l'eh-v'i-z'i-ON-ny-jeh ka-NA-ly na an-GL'I-skəm jə-zy-K'EH?

I want a bigger room.
Я хочу комнату побольше.
Ja ha-CHU KOM-na-tu pa-BOL'-sheh.

Do you serve breakfast in the morning?
Вы подаёте завтрак по утрам?
Vy pa-da-JO-t'eh ZAF-trək pa ut-RAM?

Oh, it's spacious.
О, просторно.
O, pras-TOR-nə.

My room is this way.
Моя комната здесь.
Ma-JA KOM-na-ta zd'ehs'.

Straight down the hall.
Прямо по коридору.
PR'A-mə pa ka-r'i-DO-ru.

Can you suggest a different hotel?
Вы можете предложить другой отель?
Vy MO-zheh-t'eh pr'ehd-la-ZHYT' dru-GOJ a-TEHL'?

Does the room have a safe for my valuables?
В номере есть сейф для моих ценных вещей?
V NO-m'eh-r'eh jehst' s'ehjf dl'a ma-IH TSEH-nyh v'eh-SCH'EHJ?

Please clean my room.

Пожалуйста, сделайте уборку в моей комнате.

Pa-ZHA-ləs-tə, ZD'EH-laj-t'eh u-BOR-ku v ma-JEHJ KOM-na-t'eh.

Don't disturb me, please.

Не беспокойте меня, пожалуйста.

N'eh b'ehs-pa-KOJ-t'eh m'eh-N'A, pa-ZHA-ləs-tə.

Can you wake me up at noon?

Вы можете разбудить меня в полдень?

Vy MO-zheh-t'eh raz-bu-D'IT' m'eh-N'A f POL-d'ehn'?

I would like to check out of my hotel room.

Я бы хотел/хотела выписаться из номера.

Ja by ha-T'EHL/ha-T'EH-la VY-p'i-sa-tsa iz NO-m'eh-ra.

Please increase the cleanup duty of my hotel room.

Пожалуйста, делайте уборку в моём номере чаще.

Pa-ZHA-ləs-tə, D'EH-laj-t'eh u-BOR-ku v ma-JOM NO-m'eh-r'eh CHA-sch'eh.

Is the Marriott any good?

Марриотт хороший отель?

MA-r'i-ot ha-RO-shyj a-TEHL'?

Is it expensive to stay at the Marriott?

Марриотт дорогой отель?

MA-r'i-ot da-ra-GOJ a-TEHL'?

I think our room has bedbugs.

По-моему, в нашем номере есть клопы.

Pa-MO-jeh-mu, v NA-shehm NO-m'eh-r'eh jehst' kla-PY.

Can you send an exterminator to our room?

Вы не могли бы прислать в наш номер специалиста по истреблению паразитов?

Vy n'eh mag-L'I by pr'is-LAT' v nash NO-m'ehr sp'eh-tsy-a-L'IS-ta pa is-tr'ehb-L'EH-n'i-ju pa-ra-Z'I-təf?

I need to speak to your manager.

Мне нужно поговорить с вашим менеджером.

Mn'eh NUZH-nə pa-ga-va-R'IT' s VA-shym MEH-neh-dzheh-rəm.

Do you have the number to corporate?

У вас есть номер головного офиса?

U vas jehst' NO-m'ehr ga-lav-NO-və O-f'i-sa?

Does the hotel shuttle go to the casino?

Отель предоставляет трансфер до казино?

A-TEHL' pr'eh-das-tav-L'A-jeht TRANS-f'ehr da ka-z'i-NO?

Can you call me when the hotel shuttle is on its way?

Вы не могли бы позвонить мне, когда трансфер отеля будет в пути?

Vy n'eh mag-L'I by paz-va-N'IT' mn'eh, kag-DA TRANS-f'ehr a-TEH-l'a BU-d'eht f pu-T'I?

Can we reserve this space for a party?

Мы можем забронировать это место для вечеринки?

My MO-zhem zab-ra-N'I-rə-vət' EH-tə M'EHS-tə dl'a v'eh-ch'eh-R'IN-k'i?

What is the guest limit for reserving an area?

Какое максимальное количество гостей для бронирования места для вечеринки?

Ka-KO-jeh mak-s'i-MAL'-nə-jeh ka-L'I-ch'ehs-tvə gas-T'EHJ dl'a bra-N'I-rə-va-n'i-ja M'EHS-tə dl'a v'eh-ch'eh-R'IN-k'i?

What are the rules for reserving an area?

Какие правила бронирования места для вечеринки?

Ka-K'I-jeh PRA-v'i-la bra-N'I-rə-va-n'i-ja M'EHS-ta dl'a v'eh-ch'eh-R'IN-k'i?

Can we serve or drink alcohol during our get together?

Мы можем подавать или пить алкоголь во время нашей встречи?

My MO-zhehm pa-da-VAT' I-l'i p'it' al-ka-GOL' və VR'EH-m'a NA-shehj FSTR'EH-chi?

I would like to complain about a noisy room next to us.

Я бы хотел/хотела пожаловаться на шумный номер рядом с нашим.

Ja by ha-T'EHL/ha-T'EH-la pa-ZHA-lə-və-tsa na SHUM-nyj NO-m'ehr R'A-dəm s NA-shym.

We have some personal items missing from our room.

Из нашего номера пропали некоторые личные вещи.

Iz NA-sheh-və NO-m'eh-ra pra-PA-l'i N'EH-ka-tə-ry-jeh L'ICH-ny-jeh V'EH-sch'i.

SPORTS AND EXERCISE

Can we walk faster?

Мы можем идти быстрее?

My MO-zhem i-T'I bys-TR'EH-jeh?

Do you want to go to a drag race track?

Ты хочешь пойти на гонки?

Ty HO-ch'ehsh paj-T'I na GON-k'i?

Are you taking a walk?

Ты собираешься на прогулку?

Ty sa-b'i-RA-jehsh-s'a na pra-GUL-ku?

Do you want to jog for a kilometer or two?

Не хочешь пробежаться километр или два?

N'eh HO-chesh pra-b'eh-ZHA-tsa k'i-la-M'EHTR I-l'i dva?

How about fast walking?

Как насчёт быстрой ходьбы?

Kak na-SCH'OT BYS-trəj had'-BY?

Would you like to walk with me?

Ты не хочешь прогуляться со мной?

Ty n'eh HO-chesh pra-gu-L'A-tsa sə mnoj?

He is a really good player.

Он очень хороший игрок.

On O-chehn' ha-RO-shyj ig-ROK.

I feel bad that they traded him to the other team.

Мне не нравится, что они «продали» его в другую команду.

Mn'eh n'eh NRA-v'i-tsa, shto a-N'I pra-DA-l'I jeh-VO v dru-GU-ju ka-MAN-du.

Did you see that home run?

Ты видел/видела этот гол?

Ty V'I-d'ehl/V'I-d'eh-la EH-tət gol?

I have been a fan of that team for many years.
Я фанат этой команды уже много лет.
Ja fa-NAT EH-təj ka-MAN-dy u-ZHEH MNO-gə l'eht.

Who is your favorite team?
Какая твоя любимая команда?
Ka-KA-ja tva-JA l'u-B'I-ma-ja ka-MAN-da?

Pelé is my favorite player.
Пеле — мой любимый игрок.
P'eh-L'Eh — moj l'u-B'I-myj ig-ROK.

Do you like soccer?
Ты любишь футбол?
Ty L'U-b'ish fud-BOL?

Do you watch American football?
Ты смотришь американский футбол?
Ty SMO-tr'ish a-m'eh-r'i-KAN-sk'ij fud-BOL?

Are there any games on right now?
По телевизору сейчас идут какие-нибудь игры?
Pa t'eh-l'eh-V'I-zə-ru s'eh-CHAS i-DUT ka-K'I-jeh n'i-but' IG-ry?

That was a bad call by the ref.
Решение судьи было неправильным.
R'eh-SHEH-n'i-jeh sud'-JI BY-lə n'eh-PRA-v'il'-nym.

I put a lot of money on this game.
Я поставил/поставила на эту игру много денег.
Ja pas-TA-vil/pas-TA-v'i-la na EH-tu ig-RU MNO-gə D'EH-n'ehg.

His stats have been incredible this season.
Его статистика невероятна в этом сезоне.
Jeh-VO sta-T'IS-t'i-ka n'eh-v'eh-ra-JAT-nə v EH-təm s'eh-ZO-n'eh.

Do you want to play baseball today?
Ты хочешь поиграть сегодня в бейсбол?
Ty HO-chehsh pa-i-GRAT' s'eh-VO-dn'a v b'ehjs-BOL?

Let's go to the soccer field and practice.
Давай пойдём на футбольное поле потренироваться.
Da-VAJ paj-D'OM na fut-BOL'-nə-jeh PO-l'eh pa-tr'eh-n'i-ra-VA-tsa.

I am barely working up a sweat.

Я даже не вспотел/вспотела.

Ja DA-zheh n'eh fspa-T'EHL/fspa-T'EH-la.

Let's go to the gym and lift weights.

Пойдём в тренажёрный зал покачаемся.

Paj-D'OM f tr'eh-na-ZHOR-nyj zal pa-ka-CHA-jehm-s'a.

Give me more weights.

Добавь мне дисков.

Da-BAF' mn'eh D'IS-kəf.

Take some weights off.

Сними пару дисков.

Sn'i-M'I PA-ru D'IS-kəf.

Will you spot me?

Ты мне поможешь?

Ty mn'eh pa-MO-zh'ehsh?

How long do you want to run on the treadmill?

Сколько ты хочешь бежать на беговой дорожке?

SKOL'-kə ty HO-chehsh b'eh-ZHAT' na b'eh-ga-VOJ da-ROSH-k'eh?

Is this the best gym in the area?

Это лучший тренажёрный зал в этом районе?

EH-tə LU-chshyj tr'eh-na-ZHOR-nyj zal v EH-təm ra-JO-n'eh?

Do I need a membership to enter this gym?

Мне нужен абонемент, чтобы ходить в этот тренажёрный зал?

Mn'eh NU-zhehn a-ba-n'eh-M'EHNT, SHTO-by ha-D'IT' v EH-tət tr'eh-na-ZHOR-nyj zal?

Do you have trial memberships for tourists?

У вас есть тестовый абонемент для туристов?

U vas jehst' TEHS-tə-vyj a-ba-n'eh-M'EHNT dl'a tu-R'IS-təf?

My muscles are still sore from the last workout.

Мои мышцы ещё болят после последней тренировки.

Ma-I MYSH-tsy jeh-SCH'O ba-L'AT posl'ə pas-L'EHD-n'ehj tr'eh-n'i-ROF-k'i.

Give me a second while I adjust this.

Дайте мне минутку, пока я разберусь с этим.

DAJ-t'eh mn'eh m'i-NUT-ku, pa-KA ja raz-b'eh-RUS' s EH-t'im.

Time to hit the steam room!

Пора в сауну!

Pa-RA f SA-u-nu!

You can put that in my locker.

Можешь положить это в мой шкафчик.

MO-zhehsh pa-la-ZHYT' EH-tə v moj SHKAF-chik.

I think we have to take turns on this machine.

Я думаю, мы должны заниматься на этом тренажёре по очереди.

Ja DU-ma-ju, my dal-ZHNY za-n'i-MA-tsa na EH-təm tr'eh-na-ZHO-r'eh pa O-ch'eh-r'eh-d'i.

Make sure to wipe down the equipment when you are done.

Не забудьте протереть оборудование, когда закончите.

N'eh za-BUT'-t'eh pra-t'eh-R'EHT' a-ba-RU-də-va-n'i-jeh, kag-DA za-KON-chi-t'eh.

Is there a time limit on working out here?

Время для тренировок здесь ограничено?

VR'EH-m'a dl'a tr'eh-n'i-RO-vək zd'ehs' ag-ra-N'I-ch'eh-nə?

We should enter a marathon.

Нам надо поучаствовать в марафоне.

Nam NA-də pa-u-CHAS-tvə-vət' v ma-ra-FO-n'eh.

How has your diet been going?

Как твоя диета?

Kak tva-JA d'i-JEH-ta?

Are you doing keto?

Ты соблюдаешь кето диету?

Ty sab-l'u-DA-jehsh K'EH-tə d'i-JEH-tu?

Make sure to stay hydrated while you work out.

Не забывайте пить достаточно жидкости во время тренировок.

N'eh za-by-VAJ-t'eh p'it' das-TA-təch-nə ZHYT-kəs-t'i va VR'EH-m'a tr'eh-n'i-RO-vək.

I'll go grab you a protein shake.

Я пойду возьму тебе протеиновый коктейль.

Ja paj-DU vaz'-MU t'eh-B'EH pra-t'eh-I-nə-vyj kak-T'EHJL'.

Do you want anything else? I'm buying.
Хочешь что-нибудь ещё? Я плачу.
HO-chehsh SHTO-n'i-but' jeh-SCH'O? Ja pla-CHU.

I need to buy some equipment before I play that.
Мне нужно купить кое-какое снаряжение, прежде чем играть в эту игру.
Mn'eh NUZH-nə ku-P'IT' kojeh-ka-KO-jeh sna-r'ə-ZHEH-n'i-jeh, PR'EHZH-d'eh ch'em ig-RAT' v EH-tu ig-RU.

Do you want to spar?
Хочешь провести спарринг?
HO-ch'ehsh pra-v'ehs-T'I SPA-r'ing?

Full contact sparring.
Полноконтактный спарринг.
Pol-nəkan-TAK-nyj SPA-r'ing.

Just a simple practice round.
Просто обычный тренировочный раунд.
PROS-tə a-BYCH-nyj tr'eh-n'i-RO-vəch-nyj RA-und.

Do you want to wrestle?
Хочешь побороться?
HO-chehsh pa-ba-RO-tsa?

What are the rules to play this game?
Какие правила у этой игры?
Ka-K'I-jeh PRA-v'i-la u EH-təj ig-RY?

Do we need a referee?
Нам нужен судья?
Nam NU-zhehn sud'-JA?

I don't agree with that call.
Я не согласен/согласна с этим замечанием.
Ja n'eh sag-LA-s'ehn/sag-LAS-na s EH-t'im za-m'eh-CHA-n'i-jehm.

Can we get another opinion on that score?
Мы можем узнать другое мнение по поводу этого гола?
My MO-zhehm uz-NAT' dru-GO-jeh MN'EH-n'i-jeh pa PO-və-du EH-tə-və GO-lə?

How about a game of table tennis?
Как насчёт партии в настольный теннис?
Kak nas-CH'OT PAR-t'i-i v nas-TOL'-nyj TEH-n'is?

Do you want to team up?
Вы хотите объединиться?
Vy ha-T'I-t'eh ab-jeh-d'i-N'I-tsa?

Goal!
Гол!
Gol!

Homerun!
В яблочко!
V JAB-ləch-kə!

Touchdown!
Тачдаун!
Tach-DA-un!

Score!
Очко!
Ach-KO!

On your mark, get set, go!
На старт, внимание, марш!
Na start, vn'i-MA-n'i-jeh, marsh!

Do you want to borrow my equipment?
Хочешь одолжить моё снаряжение?
HO-chehsh a-dal-ZHYT' ma-JO sna-r'a-ZHEH-n'i-jeh?

Hold the game for a second.
Остановите игру на секунду.
As-ta-na-V'I-t'eh ig-RU na s'eh-KUN-du.

I don't understand the rules of this game.
Я не понимаю правил этой игры.
Ja n'eh pa-n'i-MA-ju PRA-v'il EH-təj ig-RY.

Timeout!
Таймаут!
Tajm-AUT!

Can we switch sides?
Мы можем поменяться местами?
My MO-zhehm pa-m'eh-N'A-tsa m'ehs-TA-m'i?

There is something wrong with my equipment.
С моим снаряжением что-то не так.
S ma-IM sna-r'a-ZHEH-n'i-jehm SHTO-tə n'eh tak.

How about another game?
Сыграем ещё?
Syg-RA-jehm jeh-SCH'O?

I would like a do over of that last game.
Я бы хотел/хотела переиграть последнюю игру.
Ja by ha-T'EHL/ha-T'EH-la p'eh-r'eh-ig-RAT' pas-L'EHD-n'u-ju ig-RU.

Do you want to go golfing?
Хочешь поиграть в гольф?
HO'chehsh pa-ig-RAT' v gol'f?

Where can we get a golf cart?
Где мы можем взять гольфкар?
Gd'eh my MO-zhehm vz'at' gol'f-KAR?

Do you have your own clubs?
У тебя есть свои клюшки?
U t'eh-B'A jehst' sva-I KL'U-shk'i.

Would you like to play with my spare clubs?
Хочешь поиграть моими свободными клюшками?
HO-chehsh pa-ig-RAT' ma-I-m'I sva-BOD-ny-m'I K'LU-shka-m'i?

How many holes do you want to play?
Со сколькими лунками ты хочешь играть?
Sa SKOL'k'i-m'i LUN-kə-m'i ty HO-chehsh ig-RAT'.

Do I have to be a member of this club to play?
Я должен/должна быть членом этого клуба, чтобы играть?
Ja DOL-zhehn/dal-ZHNA byt' CHL'EH-nəm EH-tə-və KLU-ba, SHTO-by ig-RAT'?

Let me ice this down, it is sore.
Дайте мне приложить лёд, мне больно.
DAJ-t'eh mn'eh pr'i-la-ZHYT' l'od, mn'eh BOL'-nə.

I can't keep up with you, slow down.

Я не успеваю за тобой, помедленнее.

Ja n'eh us-pe-VA-ju za ta-BOJ, pa-M'EH-dl'eh-n'eh-jeh.

Let's pick up the pace a little bit.

Давай немного ускорим темп.

Da-VAJ n'ehm-NO-gə us-KO-r'im tehmp.

Do you need me to help you with that?

Тебе здесь нужна моя помощь?

T'eh-B'EH zd'ehs' nuzh-NA ma-JA PO-məsch?

Am I being unfair?

Я несправедлив/несправедлива?

Ja n'eh-spra-v'ehd-L'IF/n'eh-spra-v'ehd-L'I-va?

Let's switch teams for the next game.

Давайте поменяемся командами для следующей игры.

Da-VAJ-t'eh pa-m'eh-N'A-jehm-s'a ka-MAN-də-m'i dl'a SL'EH-du-ju-sch'ehj ig-RY.

Hand me those weights.

Подай мне те гантели.

Pa-DAJ mn'eh t'eh gan-T'EH-l'i.

THE FIRST 24 HOURS AFTER ARRIVING

When did you arrive?
Когда вы прибыли?
Kag-DA vy PR'I-by-l'i?

That was a very pleasant flight.
Полёт был очень приятным.
Pa-L'OT byl O-ch'ehn' pr'i-JAT-nym.

Yes, it was a very peaceful trip. Nothing bad happened.
Да, поездка была очень спокойной. Ничего плохого не произошло.
Da, pa-JEHS-tka by-LA O-chehn' spa-KOJ-nəj. N'i-ch'eh-VO pla-HO-və n'eh pra-i-zash-LO.

I have jetlag so need to lay down for a bit.
На мне сказывается разница в часовых поясах, так что мне нужно прилечь ненадолго.
Na mn'eh SKA-zy-va-jeh-tsa RAZ-n'i-tsa f cha-sa-VYH pa-ja-SAH, tak shto mn'eh NUZH-nə pr'i-LEHCH n'eh-na-DOL-gə.

No, that was my first time flying.
Нет, я летал/летала впервые.
N'eht, ja l'eh-TAL/l'eh-TA-la fp'ehr-VY-jeh.

When is the check-in time?
Во сколько регистрация?
Va SKOL'-kə r'eh-g'is-TRA-tsy-ja?

Do we need to get cash?
Нам нужно иметь наличные?
Nam NUZH-nə i-M'EHT' na-L'ICH-ny-jeh?

How much money do you have on you?
Сколько денег у вас с собой?
SKOL'-kə D'EH-n'ehg u vas s sa-BOJ?

How long do you want to stay here?

Сколько вы хотите пробыть здесь?

SKOL'-kə vy ha-T'I-t'eh pra-BYT' zd'ehs'?

Do we have all of our luggage?

Весь наш багаж на месте?

V'ehs' nash ba-GASH ma M'EHS-t'eh?

Let's walk around the city a bit before checking in.

Давай немного прогуляемся по городу, прежде чем зарегистрироваться.

Da-VAJ n'ehm-NO-gə pra-gu-L'A-jeh-ms'a pa GO-rə-du, PR'EH-zhd'eh ch'ehm za-r'eh-g'is-TR'I-rə-və-tsa.

When is check-in time for our hotel?

Во сколько мы должны зарегистрироваться в отеле?

Va SKOL'-kə my dal-ZHNY za-r'eh-g'is-TR'I-rə-və-tsa v a-TEH-l'eh?

I'll call the landlord and let him know we landed.

Я позвоню хозяину и сообщу ему, что мы приземлились.

Ja paz-va-N'U ha-Z'A-i-nu i sa-ap-SCH'U jeh-MU, shto my pr'i-z'ehm-L'I-l'is'.

Let's find a place to rent a car.

Давай найдём, где арендовать машину.

Da-VAJ naj-D'OM, gd'eh a'-r'ehn-da-VAT' ma-SHY-nu.

Let's walk around the hotel room and make sure it's in order.

Давай проверим гостиничный номер, чтобы убедиться, что всё в порядке.

Da-VAJ pra-V'EH-r'im gas-T'I-n'ich-nyj NO-m'ehr, SHTO-by u-b'eh-D'I-tsa, shto fs'o f pa-R'A-tk'eh.

We'll look at our apartment and make sure everything is in order.

Мы осмотрим нашу квартиру, чтобы убедиться, что всё в порядке.

My as-MO-tr'im NA-shy kvar-T'I-ru, SHTO-by u-b'eh-D'I-tsa, shto fs'o f pa-R'AT-k'eh.

THE LAST 24 HOURS BEFORE LEAVING

Where are the passports?
Где паспорта?
Gd'eh pas-par-TA?

Did you fill out the customs forms?
Вы заполнили таможенные бланки?
Vy za-POL-n'i-l'i ta-MO-zheh-ny-jeh BLAN-k'i?

Make sure to pack everything.
Не забудь всё упаковать.
N'eh za-BUT' fs'o u-pa-kə-VAT'.

Where are we going?
Куда мы едем?
Ku-DA my JEH-d'ehm?

Which flight are we taking?
Каким рейсом мы летим?
Ka-K'IM R'EHJ-sam my l'eh-T'IM?

Check your pockets.
Проверь свои карманы.
Pra-V'EHR' sva-I kar-MA-ny.

I need to declare some things for customs.
Мне нужно задекларировать некоторые вещи.
Mn'eh NUZH-nə za-d'ehk-la-R'I-rə-vat' n'eh-KA-tə-ry-jeh V'EH-schi.

No, I have nothing to declare.
Нет, мне нечего декларировать.
N'eht, mn'eh N'EH-cheh-və d'ehk-la-R'I-rə-vət'.

What is the checkout time?
Во сколько мы должны выписаться?
Va SKOL'-kə my dal-ZHNY VY-p'i-sa-tsa?

Make sure your phone is charged.
Не забудь зарядить телефон.
N'eh za-BUT' za-r'ə-D'IT' t'eh-l'eh-FON.

Is there a fee attached to this?
Есть ли плата за это?
Jehst' l'i PLA-ta za EH-tə?

Do we have any outstanding bills to pay?
Нам нужно оплатить ещё какие-нибудь счета?
Nam NUZH-nə ap-la-T'IT' jeh-SCHO ka-K'I-jeh-n'i-but' sch'eh-TA?

What time does our flight leave?
Во сколько вылетает наш рейс?
Va SKOL'-kə vy-l'eh-TA-jeht nash r'ehjs?

What time do we need to be at the airport?
Во сколько мы должны быть в аэропорту?
Va SKOL'-kə my dal-ZHNY byt' v a-eh-ra-par-TU?

How bad is the traffic going in the direction of the airport?
Насколько сильно загружена дорога в направлении аэропорта?
Nas-KOL'-kə S'IL'-nə zag-RU-zheh-na da-RO-gə v nap-rav-L'EH-n'i-i a-eh-rə-POR-ta?

Are there any detours we can take?
Мы можем поехать в объезд?
My MO-zhehm pa-JEH-hət' v ab-JEHST?

What haven't we seen from our list since we've been down here?
Что из нашего списка мы не посетили с тех пор, как приехали сюда?
Shto iz NA-sheh-və SP'IS-kə my n'eh pa-s'eh-T'I-l'i s t'ehh por, kak pr'i-JEH-ha-l'i s'u-DA?

We should really buy some souvenirs here.
Нам точно нужно купить здесь пару сувениров.
Nam TOCH-nə NUZH-nə ku-P'IT' zd'ehs' PA-ru su-v'eh-N'I-rəf.

Do you know any shortcuts that will get us there faster?
Вы знаете, как срезать дорогу, чтобы нам доехать быстрее?
Vy ZNA-j'eh-t'eh, kak SR'EH-zat' da-RO-gu, SHTO-by nam da-JEH-hət' bys-TR'EH-jeh?

GPS the location and save it.
Найди место на GPS и сохрани его.
Naj-D'I M'EHS-tə na GPS i sah-ra-n'i jeh-VO.

Are the items we're bringing back allowed on the plane?
Вещи, которые мы везём с собой отсюда, разрешено брать в самолёт?
V'EH-schi, ka-TO-ry-jeh my v'eh-Z'OM s sa-BOJ at-S'U-də, raz-r'eh-sheh-NO brat' f sa-ma-L'OT?

We should call our family back home before leaving.
Нам нужно позвонить домой семье перед отъездом.
Nam NUZH-nə paz-va-N'IT' da-MOJ s'ehm-JEH p'eh-r'ehd at-JEHZ-dəm.

Make sure the pet cage is locked.
Убедитесь, что клетка для животных закрыта.
U-b'eh-D'I-t'ehs', shto KL'EHT-ka dl'a zhy-VOT-nyh zak-RY-ta.

Go through your luggage again.
Проверь свой багаж ещё раз.
Pra-V'EHR' svoj ba-GASH jeh-SCH'O ras.

CONCLUSION

Congratulations! You have reached the end of this book and learned over **1,500** ways to express yourself in the Russian language! It is a moment to celebrate, since you are now much closer to achieving complete fluency of the Russian tongue.

However, the learning simply cannot end here – you may have unlocked a massive amount of incredibly useful day-to-day phrases that will get you anywhere you need to go, but are you prepared to use them correctly? Furthermore, will you actually remember them during your travels when faced with one of the situations we've presented in this book?

Only by continuously studying the material found in these chapters will you ever be able to summon the words and phrases encountered above, since it isn't a matter of *what* the phrases are but *how* and *when* to use them. Knowing the exact context is crucial, as well as reinforcing your knowledge with other materials.

For this reason, we have created a quick list of tips to make the most of this Russian Phrasebook and expanding your vocabulary and grasp of the Russian language:

1. **Practice every day:** You can be very good at something thanks to the gift of natural talent, but practice is the only way to *stay* good. Make sure to constantly pick up the book and read the words, saying them out loud and taking note of your mistakes so you can correct them.

2. **Read while listening:** A very popular and modern way of learning a new language is by using the RwL (reading while listening) method. It has been proven that this method can greatly boost fluency, help you ace language tests, and improve your learning in other subjects. Feel free to try out our audiobooks and other listening materials in Russian – you'll love them!

3. **Studying in groups:** It's always best to go on an adventure together – even if it's a language adventure! You'll enjoy yourself more if you can find someone who wants to learn with you. Look to friends, your partner, your family members, or colleagues for support, and maybe they can even help you make the process easier and quicker!

4. **Creating your own exercises:** This book provides you with plenty of material for your learning processes, and you will probably be happy with reading it every time you can... however, you need to increase the difficulty by looking for other words and phrases in the Russian language which you don't know the pronunciation to and trying to decipher them for yourself. Use the knowledge you've gained with previous lessons to discover entirely new words!

With that said, we have now fully concluded this Russian Phrasebook, which will surely accelerate your learning to new levels. Don't forget to follow every tip we've included and keep an eye out for our additional Russian materials.

MORE FROM LINGO MASTERY

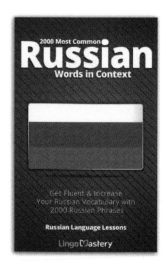

**Have you been trying to learn Russian and simply
can't find the way to expand your vocabulary?**

**Do your teachers recommend you boring textbooks
and complicated stories that you don't really understand?**

**Are you looking for a way to learn the
language quicker without taking shortcuts?**

If you answered *"Yes!"* to at least one of those previous questions, then this book is for you! We've compiled the **2000 Most Common Words in Russian,** a list of terms that will expand your vocabulary to levels previously unseen.

Did you know that — according to an important study — learning the top two thousand (2000) most frequently used words will enable you to understand up to **84%** of all non-fiction and **86.1%** of fiction literature and **92.7%** of oral speech? Those are *amazing* stats, and this book will take you even further than those numbers!

In this book:

- A detailed introduction with tips and tricks on how to improve your learning
- A list of **2000** of the most common words in Russian and their translations
- An example sentence for each word – in both Russian *and* English
- Finally, a conclusion to make sure you've learned and supply you with a final list of tips

Don't look any further, we've got what you need right here!

In fact, we're ready to turn you into a Russian speaker... are you ready to become one?

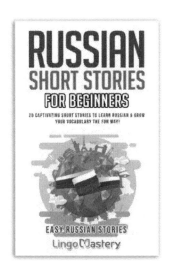

Do you know what the hardest thing for a Russian learner is?

Finding *PROPER* reading material that they can handle…which is precisely the reason we've written this book!

Teachers love giving out tough, expert-level literature to their students, books that present many new problems to the reader and force them to search for words in a dictionary every five minutes — it's not entertaining, useful or motivating for the student at all, and many soon give up on learning at all!

In this book we have compiled 20 easy-to-read, compelling and fun stories that will allow you to expand your vocabulary and give you the tools to improve your grasp of the wonderful Russian tongue.

How **Russian Short Stories for Beginners** works:

- Each story is interesting and entertaining with realistic dialogues and day-to-day situations.
- The summaries follow a synopsis in Russian and in English of what you just read, both to review the lesson and for you to see if you understood what the tale was about.
- At the end of those summaries, you'll be provided with a list of the most relevant vocabulary involved in the lesson, as well as slang and sayings that you may not have understood at first glance!

- Finally, you'll be provided with a set of tricky questions in Russian, providing you with the chance to prove that you learned something in the story. Don't worry if you don't know the answer to any — we will provide them immediately after, but no cheating!

We want you to feel comfortable while learning the tongue; after all, no language should be a barrier for you to travel around the world and expand your social circles!

So look no further! Pick up your copy of **Russian Short Stories for Beginners** and level up your Russian *right now*!

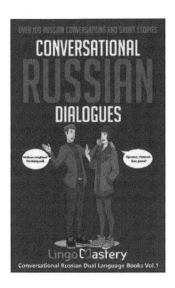

Is conversational Russian turning a little too tricky for you? Do you have no idea how to order a meal or book a room at a hotel?

If your answer to any of the previous questions was 'Yes', then this book is for you!

If there's even been something tougher than learning the grammar rules of a new language, it's finding the way to speak with other people in that tongue. Any student knows this – we can try our best at practicing, but you always want to avoid making embarrassing mistakes or not getting your message through correctly.

"How do I get out of this situation?" many students ask themselves, to no avail, but no answer is forthcoming.

Until now.

We have compiled **MORE THAN ONE HUNDRED** conversational Russian stories for beginners along with their translations, allowing new Russian speakers to have the necessary tools to begin studying how to set a meeting, rent a car or tell a doctor that they don't feel well. We're not wasting time here with conversations that don't go anywhere: if you want to know how to solve problems (while learning a ton of Russian along the way, obviously), this book is for you!

How Conversational Russian Dialogues works:

- Each new chapter will have a fresh, new story between two people who wish to solve a common, day-to-day issue that you will surely encounter in real life.
- An Russian version of the conversation will take place first, followed by an English translation. This ensures that you fully understood just what it was that they were saying.
- Before and after the main section of the book, we shall provide you with an introduction and conclusion that will offer you important strategies, tips and tricks to allow you to get the absolute most out of this learning material.
- That's about it! Simple, useful and incredibly helpful; you will NOT need another conversational Russian book once you have begun reading and studying this one!

We want you to feel comfortable while learning the tongue; after all, no language should be a barrier for you to travel around the world and expand your social circles!

So look no further! Pick up your copy of Conversational Russian Dialogues and start learning Russian right now!

Printed in Great Britain
by Amazon